This book is an important guide for those who seek justice for all people, including the unborn and vulnerable women facing excruciating choices. In *The New Fight for Life*, Benjamin Watson offers a thoughtful way forward in the battle over abortion. He brings to the forefront the call for holistic advocacy for life, from the womb to the tomb.

KATRINA JACKSON
Louisiana state senator

Benjamin Watson helps us see past the politics and hostility of this issue to better understand the factors that created these barriers and how to come together, dismantle them, and chart a new path forward. He makes a winsome case for having a holistic view of life as we advocate for the vulnerable and fight for justice with compassion and understanding.

ELIZABETH GRAHAM
CEO of Stand for Life

My good friend Benjamin Watson has given us a balanced work that uniquely weds the case for pro-life with the call for justice, both inside and outside the church. His unique voice in this excellent literary call for a righteous and compassionate fight for life is a must-read for all those who love God, love people, and care about our culture.

DR. TONY EVANS
President of The Urban Alternative and senior pastor of Oak Cliff Bible Fellowship

In close to two decades of pro-life work, I've never read a book like *The New Fight for Life*. This book is an answer to my prayers. I've continually heard from people who value the lives of the unborn but question whether the pro-life movement cares about Black lives beyond babies. This book shows we care, as it thoroughly addresses multiple justice issues impacting our community. It brilliantly weaves together history with proposed action steps that can lead us to victory during this post-*Roe* future. It's incredibly rare to find a book that dares to tackle abortion, systemic racism, and societal issues with compassion, faith, and inspiring lessons from the football field. It's a book I can't wait to get into the hands of my husband and others looking for resources they can identify with. *The New Fight for Life* is sure to ignite a fire in its readers, leading them to compassionate and sustained action.

CHRISTINA MARIE BENNETT
Live Action News correspondent

This book puts the "pro" back into "pro-life." Benjamin Watson's vision of human dignity is consistent and positive, never a proxy for culture wars or power politics. Here he models for us how to love and protect life—that of vulnerable children, their mothers, and everyone else.

RUSSELL MOORE
Editor in chief of *Christianity Today*

Thriving movements innovate, adjust to new dynamics, and anticipate oncoming obstacles, all while maintaining core convictions. In *The New Fight for Life*, Watson insightfully calls the pro-life movement to this work by challenging it to reimagine itself with a deeper commitment to justice and more faithful engagement on race.

JUSTIN E. GIBONEY
President of AND Campaign

Although history can be a great teacher, we have been poor students. Watson helps us remember not only our history but also our calling to confront the root causes of abortion. Watson's personal witness calls us to conversion and action. For those who want to end abortion, this book serves as an important guide.

GLORIA PURVIS
Author, commentator, host, and executive producer of *The Gloria Purvis Podcast*

In *The New Fight for Life*, Benjamin Watson examines the biggest question our country is facing as we debate the issue of abortion: How can we balance the need to protect innocent lives and also respect and protect the women who have to make these difficult decisions? Benjamin looks at all sides of this issue and, as he always does, gives us thoughtful answers from a biblical perspective.

TONY DUNGY
Christian speaker, author, and former NFL coach

Every Millennial and Gen Zer in America needs this book—by far one of the most important reads for this time, season, and generation. It tells the complete, unfiltered, and honest truth! This book fills a hole in an extensive market of literature. We as Black Americans have gone so long being spoken for, neglected, and used as talking points. Now there is an adequate pro-life point of view from the lenses of *us*. I feel a personal connection within my heart, passion, and culture mirrored on each page of *The New Fight for Life*.

TRENEÉ McGEE
Connecticut state representative

For decades I have spent long and fruitful hours dialoguing with pro-life advocates as well as proponents of racial justice. Both causes are close to God's heart, and I have often regretted that those who see one of these causes clearly are often blind to the other. I don't know anyone more insightful and articulate on these issues than my friends Ben and Kirsten Watson, who beautifully model a kind, thoughtful commitment to both pro-life justice and racial justice. There are things in this book that may offend some political liberals and things that may offend some political conservatives. Readers who want to learn and grow should suspend judgment and prayerfully and nondefensively listen. If you do, you may find that you agree with more than you expected to and that you can disagree with parts while being enriched by the whole. This is the kind of book that can lead us beyond shallow political slogans and stereotypes that fit on bumper stickers or on Twitter but are out of place in intelligent, respectful dialogue. The post-*Roe* era we're in now is a time to ask God to open our hearts and minds to what matters to him.

I believe he has raised up Ben Watson to be a voice for two interwoven causes that should be simultaneously embraced. I highly recommend *The New Fight for Life*.

RANDY ALCORN
Author of *Heaven, If God Is Good, Happiness,* and *Pro-Choice or Pro-Life?*

Benjamin Watson's lived experience as a Black man in America has given him unique insights into how oppression can come in many different forms—from blatant racism and violence against Black and Brown people to the more subtle and insidious poisoned apple of "choice" being disguised as a gift to his community. While many in the pro-life movement work to prune back the branches of abortion, Watson demands that we finally, once and for all, pull it up by its toxic root. In *The New Fight for Life*, he explains how the seeds of systemic racism were planted hundreds of years ago to exploit and eradicate people like him. Now it has led many to unknowingly feast on its tainted fruits . . . because when you're starving, even poisoned apples can seem like sustenance. Watson's work implores us to join him in planting a new tree—a tree of life—that will ultimately bear righteous and just fruit for generations to come.

DESTINY HERNDON-DE LA ROSA
President and founder of New Wave Feminists

Benjamin will encourage your faith, challenge your advocacy for life, and bless you with soul-stirring truths. I'm honored to read this!

LECRAE
Author and Grammy Award–winning artist

Benjamin Watson's courageous and relentless advocacy on behalf of children, mothers, and families is an inspiration to millions. *The New Fight for Life* encourages and challenges our movement to not only abolish legal abortion but fight to ensure that every mother and father has the resources and support they need to embrace and successfully raise their children. Ben's practical advice and thoughtful, wise, winsome stories are much-needed fuel for this next chapter of our era's most urgent fight for human rights.

LILA ROSE
President and founder of Live Action

THE NEW FIGHT FOR LIFE

TYNDALE
MOMENTUM®

A Tyndale nonfiction imprint

THE NEW FIGHT FOR LIFE

ROE, RACE
& A PRO-LIFE
COMMITMENT
TO JUSTICE

BENJAMIN WATSON

WITH CAROL TRAVER

Visit Tyndale online at tyndale.com.

Visit Tyndale Momentum online at tyndalemomentum.com.

Visit Benjamin Watson online at thewatsonseven.com.

Tyndale, Tyndale's quill logo, *Tyndale Momentum*, and the Tyndale Momentum logo are registered trademarks of Tyndale House Ministries. Tyndale Momentum is a nonfiction imprint of Tyndale House Publishers, Carol Stream, Illinois.

The New Fight for Life: Roe, Race, and a Pro-Life Commitment to Justice

Designed by Libby Dykstra

Published in association with the literary agency of Legacy, LLC, 501 N. Orlando Avenue, Suite #313-348, Winter Park, FL 32789.

For information about special discounts for bulk purchases, please contact Tyndale House Publishers at csresponse@tyndale.com, or call 1-855-277-9400.

Library of Congress Cataloging-in-Publication Data

A catalog record for this book is available from the Library of Congress.

ISBN 978-1-4964-8143-6 HC
ISBN 978-1-4964-8144-3 SC

Printed in the United States of America

29	28	27	26	25	24	23
7	6	5	4	3	2	1

For my children and my children's children

There comes a point where we need to stop just pulling people out of the river. We need to go upstream and find out why they're falling in.

DESMOND TUTU

CONTENTS

Foreword by Cherilyn Holloway *xv*
Author's Note *xxi*

WE NEED TO TALK

I first met Benjamin Watson in 2019. I was at a women's pro-life conference in New Orleans that I did *not* want to go to. It's not that I'm not pro-life. But I'm pro-life in a way that's different from most other pro-lifers I meet at these events.

While most people I'd met in the pro-life community at the time acknowledged the connection between abortion and race, few (if any) were talking about *why*. As the executive director of a pregnancy center, I knew how much things like the wage gap, food deserts, and disparities in the legal system, the educational system, and the housing market factor into women's decisions when it comes to abortion. But I couldn't seem to find anyone else who was willing to address these topics, let alone talk about how we might fix them.

We all valued life, and we all wanted to advocate for those who couldn't speak up for themselves. We just had different ideas about what that looked like. And because of our differences, I often felt like I was on the outside looking in.

The general approach was more targeted, focusing almost exclusively on protecting and defending the baby in the womb. And while I agree with that wholeheartedly, for me, being pro-life also means providing justice for the baby's mother, the baby's father, and, for that matter, everyone else who is made in the image of God—from the womb to the tomb, in all areas of life.

Often when I spoke at gatherings like this, I was told that I was diluting the message. But as a Black woman who has endured the emotional upheaval of two abortion decisions myself, I have a different vantage point. It's not enough simply to convince a young woman to keep her baby. We also have to make sure that woman has the ongoing financial and emotional support she needs to parent her child successfully.

Many women mistakenly believe they have no other option besides abortion because they think that they can't afford to raise a child or that they won't be able to finish school or that they won't be able to pay for childcare so they can work. A more holistic approach goes beyond just convincing them to keep their babies and helps them knock down the barriers that make them consider abortion in the first place.

For example, there are organizations that provide mothers with diapers, baby wipes, clothes, formula, and other necessary supplies free of charge. Many high schools offer GED programs. Many college campuses offer married/family housing. And some companies help employees pay for day care. There are grants, scholarships, and local faith-based and government-assisted programs that help vulnerable women and children get the help they need.

Overturning *Roe* made the right to an abortion unconstitutional. But when women are provided with options so they no longer feel as though they have to give up their child, they can get to a place where they see their pregnancy not as the end of the world but as a new beginning. Only then will abortion be, as Benjamin says, unthinkable and unnecessary. With all these options in play, not only does a woman not *have* to choose abortion, but why *would* she?

———————

As I made my way through the convention center that morning, I was anxious to find Destiny, the friend who had convinced me to come in the first place.

"Where are you?" I texted her.

A few seconds later, she responded, "I'm doing an interview."

That made sense. Destiny was a rock star at events like this. Her organization, New Wave Feminists, had been featured in newspapers, magazines, and news shows across the nation. Someone always wanted to speak with her.

"They want to talk to you next."

Now that made no sense. Why would anyone want to talk to me?

"Very funny," I texted back. "Just let me know when you're done."

"I'm serious," she replied. "They really want to talk to you."

I craned my neck to see over the crowd, looking for Destiny's trademark purple hair. I found her standing in the lobby talking to a man I didn't recognize. As soon as I approached, he introduced himself as Jason Jones.

"If you're available at 1:30," he said, "I'd like you to be interviewed by Benjamin Watson."

As an Ohio native and a lifelong Browns fan, I knew who Benjamin Watson was. What he was doing there and why he wanted to talk with me, I had no idea.

I later found out that Jason and Benjamin were recording interviews for a documentary they were making called *Divided Hearts of America.*

After Jason introduced me to Benjamin, we started talking about the need for a more holistic approach to abortion. The next thing I knew, we were in a deep dive into eugenics and how the Black community has been deliberately targeted by the abortion industry. The conversation got so intense that the director had to usher us to the official set and mic us up while we were still talking.

It was exhilarating. For the first time since I'd entered the pro-life space, I finally felt like someone got what I was talking about.

There's nothing wrong with having different ideas about how to solve a complex problem. The trouble comes when we fail to take other people's viewpoints into consideration. We need to be willing to engage with those who think differently from us and who have had different experiences so we can understand why we each believe what we believe and figure out a way forward. We don't have to agree with one another about everything, but we have a responsibility to educate ourselves and to learn from one another.

As you'll soon discover, Benjamin is a student of history, and like me, he loves research, facts, and figures. He is also a man of integrity who speaks from a firm biblical foundation resulting from decades of walking with the Lord. And people listen to him. They might not agree with everything he says, but they listen because of his witness.

In this book, Benjamin paints a vivid, fact-driven picture for people who genuinely want to learn more about how we can best advocate for the vulnerable and why abortion disproportionately affects the Black community. Only then will we be able to stop shouting at one another from across the divide and start creating bridges.

And we have *got* to start creating bridges.

We need to create bridges that help get people out of poverty. We need to create bridges to help women facing unplanned pregnancies leave abusive relationships, finish school, find well-paying jobs, and raise their children in safe, healthy neighborhoods. We need to create bridges that make abortion unthinkable and unnecessary.

I learned a lot from Benjamin at that conference, and I hope you will learn from him as well.

Thank you for joining us in this new fight for life. I can't promise you it will be easy. But I can promise you it will be worth it.

Cherilyn Holloway
FOUNDER OF PRO-BLACK PRO-LIFE

AUTHOR'S NOTE

While this book is not written from a particular political viewpoint, parts of it have policy implications. Some of these implications will likely resonate more with political conservatives, and some with political liberals. It's natural to react defensively to ideas that we associate with another political viewpoint, but wherever you lean on the political spectrum, I hope you'll reserve immediate judgment and consider whether there are some action steps and policies on the pages ahead that just might work if we give them a chance.

Additionally, while race has been a defining concept in this republic, I hope for a day when we are all considered simply human. We are one race, not many. Race is a social construct, largely based on physical characteristics or loose ancestry, that has no scientific or genetic basis. However, racism—the discrimination, exploitation, and abuse based on this false construct—is real and has devastating consequences. For that reason, I talk about race (including Black and white) in this work—not because I believe there are different races of people but because in our social context, this is how we best acknowledge, repair, and confront the damage of racism in our culture.

THE END OF THE BEGINNING

The best way for pro-life Americans to view the reversal of Roe
is not as the beginning of the end of abortion in the United States,
but rather as the end of the beginning of a long struggle to remake our
nation into a culture that is far more hospitable to mother and child.

DAVID FRENCH

On Friday, June 24, 2022, my wife, Kirsten, and I were getting ready to fly to Dallas to speak at Together '22. The two-day event was organized by Nick Hall, the founder of Pulse, an evangelism movement aimed at reaching young people all over the world for Christ.

I met Nick in 2016 in Washington, DC, when he gathered hundreds of thousands of people on the National Mall for a historic day of unified worship and prayer. Now, six years later, he was commemorating the fiftieth anniversary of the 1972 Explo, when Billy Graham preached at—of all places—the Cotton Bowl.

Together '22 was an outdoor event, and Texas was in the middle of a historic heat wave, having already stared down fourteen straight days of one hundred–plus degree temperatures. With seven kids at home, we knew it would have to be a quick fly-in-and-fly-out event for us. But once Nick told me the venue, I just couldn't say no.

I'd never been to the Cotton Bowl before, but my dad played a football game there once when he was studying at the University of Maryland, and he has worn his Cotton Bowl ring every day since. Well, *almost* every day since.

I have no recollection of this, but legend has it that when I was little, I took Daddy's Cotton Bowl ring and flushed it down the toilet, so the one he currently wears is a replica. I don't know whether this story is true, but with seven kids of my own at home, you'd better believe I keep my Super Bowl ring under lock and key.

At any rate, I'd always wanted to see the stadium, and Daddy once told me he'd accepted Christ while watching a Billy Graham crusade on TV in 1972—possibly that very event—so the nostalgia factor alone made the trip too good to pass up.

Much to Kirsten's chagrin, I've always been a last-minute packer, so while her bag was already sitting by the front door, I was still rummaging around the bedroom trying to get my act together. We weren't going to be gone long, so I just threw a change of clothes and my One Year Bible into an overnight bag and headed to the kitchen to grab a quick bite to eat.

As usual, the kitchen was a hive of activity, with kids scattered everywhere. Yet somehow Kirsten was the picture of serenity in the middle of it all, rinsing off the last of the breakfast dishes and loading them into the dishwasher.

"Hurry up, babe," she called over her shoulder. "As soon as the sitter gets here, we've got to go."

I took a quick glance at my phone to check the time, and then, sheerly out of habit, I clicked over to Twitter. There it was: "BREAKING: U.S. SUPREME COURT OVERTURNS ROE V. WADE."[1]

With my feet frozen in place, I quickly scrolled down.

"Dobbs opinion makes it official: Roe and Casey overturned."[2]

"26 states are expected to ban or severely restrict abortion rights in wake of the Supreme Court's ruling overturning Roe v. Wade."[3]

"Oh, my God," I said, half praying, half in shock. "It's over."

"What's over, baby?" Kirsten asked.

I looked at her, stunned. "*Roe*. They just overturned it."

"Are you serious?" She rushed over to look at my phone, and we both stared at the screen in silent disbelief.

Don't get me wrong—we were thrilled. Like millions of others, we'd been praying for this day for years. And like millions of others, we'd been tipped off that this day was coming.

Just seven weeks earlier, Politico.com had published a leaked draft opinion from Justice Samuel Alito. In it, Alito stated, "*Roe* was egregiously wrong from the start. Its reasoning was exceptionally weak, and the decision has had damaging consequences. And far from bringing about a national settlement of the abortion issue, *Roe* and *Casey* have enflamed debate and deepened division." He went on to declare that both

"*Roe* and *Casey* must be overruled. The Constitution makes no reference to abortion, and no such right is implicitly protected by any constitutional provision."[4]

He wasn't wrong about that. Even Ruth Bader Ginsburg, who had always been a fierce advocate for women's rights, had taken issue with the constitutionality of *Roe v. Wade*, commenting that Roe "ventured too far in the change it ordered and presented an incomplete justification for its action."[5]

"It is time," Alito concluded, "to heed the Constitution and return the issue of abortion to the people's elected representatives."[6]

It seemed too good to be true. For one thing, leaks like this—especially about rulings as incendiary as *Roe v. Wade*—just didn't happen. And even if it was true, I had a hard time believing our culture was in a place where a ruling like this could even happen.

A lot of people say that law is downstream of culture, and I think that's partly true. But I also think that law informs what's acceptable in a culture. Take same-sex marriage, for instance. Before 2015, ballot measures to restrict same-sex marriage routinely passed by popular vote in several states. But after the Supreme Court established the constitutional right for same-sex couples to marry in *Obergefell v. Hodges*, polling numbers on the constitutionality of gay marriage showed a significant trend upward.[7] Simply put, people become more accepting of what has been codified into law.

In the case of abortion, which had been legal for almost fifty years, the culture—though deeply divided—seemed to have grown accustomed to it.

Granted, the lower courts had been chipping away at the constitutionality of abortion for years. The *Planned Parenthood v. Casey* decision of 1992, for example, overruled the trimester framework established under *Roe v. Wade* in favor of viability analysis. Then in 2003, President George W. Bush signed into law the Partial Birth Abortion Ban Act, effectively prohibiting late-term abortions.[8] So by the time the *Dobbs v. Jackson Women's Health Organization* case came along in 2022, there had been enough incremental shifts to make *Roe v. Wade* vulnerable. But even with the recent appointments of Brett Kavanaugh and Amy Coney Barrett shifting the balance, I really didn't think the Supreme Court would be willing to rock the proverbial boat.

And yet, as I read the leaked draft, I couldn't help but wonder, *What if it's true?*

As the full weight of the decision washed over me, I felt a multitude of emotions. I thought about all the people I'd met since God had swept Kirsten and me onto this pro-life journey—people who had dedicated their lives to caring for the women who walked through the doors of pregnancy centers, fighting for the rights of the preborn in courtrooms, and advocating for the needs of women and children in underserved communities across the country—and about all the lives that would be saved now that *Roe* had been overturned. It was a lot to take in.

———————

Within minutes of the announcement going live, texts started pouring in from friends and colleagues:

Roe is done!

So relieved they didn't back off the draft opinion!

Congratulations on a huge win! This was our Super Bowl today!

Thank you all for having the courage to stand for life and be the wind that brought the change!

Headlines and hallelujahs continued to flit across the screen, cementing that the decision we'd been waiting for and praying for was finally a reality. As much as I appreciated everyone's excitement and enthusiasm, all I could think was, *Now what?*

My mind began to recall numerous conversations I'd had with women and men from various viewpoints about the complexities surrounding abortion. While the distinction between choosing life and death is, in my mind, abundantly clear, I also knew about the web of relational, economic, and emotional factors that were not likely to be addressed with the repealing of *Roe*.

Unfortunately, Kirsten and I were too rushed to unpack the matter more that morning. But once we were in the air and Kirsten had fallen asleep, I pulled my One Year Bible out of my bag to spend some much-needed time in God's Word. I wish I could say that I'm always up-to-date, but as sometimes happens, I had fallen a few days behind in my daily readings. Now more than ever, I felt the need to re-center myself. I flipped to where I'd left off—June 21—and for the second time that morning, I was stunned into silence.

The day's reading was Psalm 139. I knew those verses like the back of my hand.

> You made all the delicate, inner parts of my body
>> and knit me together in my mother's womb.
> Thank you for making me so wonderfully complex!
>> Your workmanship is marvelous—how well I
>>> know it.
> You watched me as I was being formed in utter
>> seclusion,
>> as I was woven together in the dark of the womb.
> You saw me before I was born.
>> Every day of my life was recorded in your book.
> Every moment was laid out
>> before a single day had passed.

PSALM 139:3-18

I couldn't believe it. It felt like God was directly affirming this fight for life that people had been pouring their lives into for so many years. It seemed he was speaking directly to me, reminding me of his heart for the most vulnerable among us and urging me on in the fight.

Something like this had happened to me one other time. It was back in 2020, when I was flying to Florida to record a program about faith and football with Coach Tony Dungy. We were talking about the intersection of faith and justice, and normally I'd be all over that. However, we were only a few months removed from the murder of George Floyd, and the latest reckoning with ongoing racism across the country was still sky-high. I was a little nervous about finding a way to faithfully and honestly delve into such a traumatic topic.

Then I opened my One Year Bible and found Psalm 16:8 waiting for me, like a balm:

> I have set the LORD continually before me;
>   because he is at my right hand, I will not be shaken.
>   (ESV)

The title of our discussion that day, which we'd chosen months prior, was "Unshaken." In that still moment, it felt like God saw all we were carrying and was reminding me that he was my true foundation, my refuge in a discouraging time. At 36,000 feet in the air, I could sense the Spirit giving me courage to speak truth and grace into this situation. We really do serve an amazing Lord.

———————

By the time we left Dallas that evening, the online frenzy had reached fever pitch. While Kirsten and I were onstage talking about the joys of parenting and the importance of fostering a sense of justice and empathy in our kids, people all over the country were taking to social media to celebrate, debate, grieve, and denounce the Supreme Court's decision.

The spectrum of emotions couldn't have been wider.

On one end were the pro-lifers, who were ecstatic, posting

videos and selfies outside the Supreme Court, cheering, hugging, and crying tears of joy and relief.

On the other end were members of the pro-choice movement, many of whom were understandably incensed. Some felt betrayed. They firmly believed their constitutional rights had been violated by the decision. Others were fearful that this might lead to the reversal of other rulings, especially those that protected rights to contraception, interracial relationships, and same-sex marriage. The anger and anxiety were palpable.

And the vitriol was by no means limited to the Internet. In the days and weeks following the leak, protesters had been vandalizing and, in some cases, setting fire to pro-life offices and pregnancy resource centers across the country. Fencing was erected around the Supreme Court Building to keep protesters at bay. Several justices and their families had received death threats, and one irate activist showed up outside Justice Kavanaugh's house brandishing a gun.

Amid the chaos, others took a more measured approach. One of these voices was from Dr. Tony Evans, who celebrated the victory for life but also encouraged people to show compassion to those who disagreed with the ruling. He wrote, "It is time for God's people to lead the way in promoting a 'Whole Life Agenda,' from the womb to the tomb. . . . While doing so, may we never forget to show compassion to those who have experienced abortion as well as kindness to those who believe differently than we do on this issue. . . . We, as the body of Christ, should come alongside those in need through spiritual and tangible support."[9]

Likewise, Destiny Herndon-De La Rosa, who founded

New Wave Feminists, a pro-life group advocating for new mothers and mothers-to-be, tempered her tearful celebration with a reminder to other pro-life supporters that there is still more work to be done.

"Legally, I understand [this] is a very, very big deal," Herndon-De La Rosa said. "The systems that are currently in place are not set up to support women in the future. And that is a really, really scary thing. . . . A terrified woman who is in a desperate situation, she doesn't care what her congressman thinks about abortion. . . . She doesn't even really care if it's legal, because she feels absolutely trapped and terrified." She went on to say that the only antidote is to change these systems so a woman's life "is not over with an unintended pregnancy. . . . And that child is going to grow up and thrive, not just survive, because it is living below the poverty line with no access to education or health care or any of these other things that are vital for their development."[10]

Aside from those who were threatening violence and shouting obscenities, I felt for all of them.

I felt a sense of solemnity for those who felt as though they had been assaulted by the court's decision.

I felt compassion for the women who were legitimately frightened and felt as though they had lost their autonomy.

And I felt a deep sense of appreciation for those like Evans and Herndon-De La Rosa, who were able to see past the politics and the hostility to the humanity underneath, recognizing that the court's ruling—encouraging as it was—was just the first step in what is still a long and arduous journey ahead.

This book is about that journey.

There's no question that June 24, 2022, was a day to

be celebrated, but as political commentator and columnist David French rightly pointed out, "The simple truth is that if the pro-life movement wants to *end* abortion, it has to do much more work than merely *banning* abortion."[11]

In fact, abortion hasn't been banned. The decision has simply been passed on to the states, where a patchwork of abortion laws will undoubtedly create a precarious web of state-by-state regulation for years to come.

Women will still have unintended pregnancies and seek solutions. And the 76 percent of abortive mothers who claim they would prefer to parent if their circumstances were different will still face barriers that act as roadblocks to life.[12]

Black women in particular face unique challenges, as disparities in health, wealth, housing, employment, and education make the Black community disproportionately susceptible to the stain of abortion.

As individuals and as a nation, we need to better understand the factors that created these barriers and work together to dismantle them. In doing so, we'll create new pathways for life.

As believers, we must commit ourselves to not just advocating for preborn children in the womb but supporting both mother and child—before, during, and after birth.

As a church, we need to become a safe haven, a refuge, a place where the most vulnerable can turn—not just for spiritual help, but for emotional, material, and financial support too.

We need to chart a new path forward.

For half a century, we have fought to protect the sanctity

of human life. The battle over the constitutionality of *Roe v. Wade* may be over, but now a new fight has begun.

It's not a fight over political partisanship or constitutional constructs. It's a fight for justice—for the preborn, for the poor, and for everyone who bears the image of God.

It's a fight not just to return the debate over abortion back to the states but to create a culture where abortion is unthinkable and unnecessary.

It's a fight that will spill out of the courtrooms and into the churches, schools, and underserved neighborhoods of red and blue states alike.

I believe we *can* make abortion both unthinkable and unnecessary, but it's going to take all of us working together. It's not enough to place legal restrictions on abortion. Our higher, more complete calling must be to address the factors that drive women to choose abortion by removing the obstacles that stand in the way of choosing life. We must dismantle and make right a protracted history of economic marginalization and oppression.

The path ahead will be a steep one. But I believe it will be worth the climb. Because nothing is more worthwhile or more sacred than life.

CHAPTER 1

THE ELEPHANT IN THE ROOM

I would unite with anybody to do right; and with nobody to do wrong.

FREDERICK DOUGLASS

During my sixteen seasons in the NFL, I had the privilege of playing under some of the most accomplished head coaches in the game: Bill Belichick, Sean Payton, and John Harbaugh. Each had his own unique style and strengths, but one thing they all had in common was that none of them had a problem calling people out when they made a mistake. This was especially true of Bill Belichick.

There were times we would beat a team handily, sometimes by as many as thirty points, and the ongoing joke among my teammates would be, "What is Bill gonna fuss at us for tomorrow?" It didn't matter that we won or that we'd played a nearly flawless game—Bill was always able to pinpoint something that could have been done better.

Whether you were Tom Brady or the fifty-third man on the roster, if you did something wrong at practice or in a game, you would hear about it—often in front of everyone at a team meeting. Bill held every player on the team to the same high standard, no exceptions and no excuses.

So in the spirit of Coach Belichick, let's jump right in and acknowledge the elephant in the room. What business does a retired football player have speaking into the pro-life discussion?

It's all right. I get that question a lot, and while I realize many people consider this to be a women's issue, there are several reasons that I, as a man, have joined the ranks of those speaking into it.

For one thing, there are currently seven children (and holding) in the Watson household, each one of whom has forty-six chromosomes, twenty-three of which they got from my wife, Kirsten, and twenty-three of which they got from me. So from a strictly biological standpoint, men have an equal share in the procreation of every child.

Also—while I am by no means saying this is right—historically speaking, when it comes to politics and the law, men have held the majority of the power. Case in point: there have been 115 Supreme Court justices in US history, and all but seven of them have been white men.[1] Women didn't even hold a seat on the Supreme Court until Sandra Day O'Connor was confirmed in 1981, and there was not a Black woman represented until 2022, when Ketanji Brown Jackson became the first Black female justice in the Court's 232-year history.[2] It was seven men who voted *Roe v. Wade* into law in 1973, and five men and one woman who voted to overturn it in 2022.

I'm not trying to quell the voice of a woman speaking out on her own behalf. It's vital that women *do* advocate for themselves. But given that it's still predominantly men making the decisions, it seems to me that the most effective way to even the playing field is for men with like-minded ideologies to advocate for equality and justice along with and on behalf of women.

In many ways and for many reasons, men have championed abortion on demand in this country. They—*we*—have led the campaign to legalize this practice, harming women along the way, framing the unnatural as choice and freedom while ultimately seeking to benefit our own interests and protect our own passivity. It was a man, Dr. Alan Guttmacher, who first introduced abortion to Planned Parenthood.[3]

Too often, men have remained silent on topics that matter most, believing the common assertions that abortion is a women's issue. I have even encountered men who claim abortion is a necessary good to protect against future suffering or to keep other social ills at bay.

But as a man, I take very seriously the words written in Proverbs 31. Most people are familiar with the description of the Proverbs 31 woman, but earlier in the chapter, the author (King Lemuel) describes what his mother taught him. I suppose you could say this is what it means to be a Proverbs 31 man:

> Speak up for those who cannot speak for themselves;
>   ensure justice for those being crushed.
> Yes, speak up for the poor and helpless,
>   and see that they get justice.

PROVERBS 31:8-9

Isaiah 1:17 says, "Learn to do good; seek justice, correct oppression; bring justice to the fatherless, plead the widow's case" (ESV). Over and over in Scripture, God challenges us to protect widows, foreigners, the young, and the vulnerable. In fact, the truth of the gospel, in its totality, challenges each one of us to humbly ask God to show us places where we can make a difference.[4]

To that end, the issue of abortion is very much intertwined with others of equal importance to me, like poverty, racism, and the trafficking of children. The way I see it, these are all matters of justice.

Over the course of my career, Kirsten and I have been introduced to individuals and organizations on the front lines of some of the worst ongoing human rights violations in the world today. Through those partnerships, I've seen firsthand how poverty, inequality, fear, and desperation can push people into unthinkable choices.

I traveled to the Lebanon-Syria border in the spring of 2017 with a pastor-friend of mine to witness the impact of the war in Syria. Hundreds of thousands of refugees had fled the violence, leaving behind their homes and possessions. We met with Lebanese pastors who had opened their church doors to families fleeing violence and visited primary schools where children were trying to continue their education in an unfamiliar land. I remember seeing a student's drawing taped on the wall, depicting him and his family running from tanks and bombs.

Sitting on the floor in the primitive conditions of a tent settlement, I spoke to a father about his harrowing experience. His wife sat by his side as their children peered through the sheet that served as a door.

Recalling the dangerous journey to safety across the border, he said through our interpreter, "As a father, I just want my family to be safe. We go to sleep hoping we will wake up back home. But we don't know if we will ever return."

My heart and mind drifted thousands of miles away to my own family and how, like him, I would willingly endure extreme hardship to keep them safe. No matter the cause of suffering—war, sexual abuse, food poverty, or discrimination—human suffering should upset us, and even offend us.

So while a lot of people define pro-life as protecting the preborn, I believe being pro-life means caring about life, period, and recognizing that *everyone* has the right to flourish and be protected, regardless of age, ethnicity, gender, or socioeconomic standing.

To echo pro-life activist Cherilyn Holloway, being pro-life means that "we care about the life that is in the womb, but we also care about the man on the street. We also care about these children and where they're getting their education and health care from and Grandma and Grandpa who are entering end-of-life care and that they're treated with dignity and respect. . . . These are all whole-life issues for us."[5]

Simply put, every life bears the image of God, so every life has value. For me, being pro-life means advocating for *every* life—especially those who cannot advocate for themselves.

There's one more reason I choose to lend my voice to this issue.

Since I retired from the NFL in 2020, I've been doing weekly game analysis for the SEC Network. Normally I'm in the studio in Charlotte, but when the College Football Playoff rolls around, I get to go on the road to recap the games on-site.

In December of 2021, I was in Miami for the Orange Bowl, and the network set us up in the main concourse so they could show fans walking by as we talked about the game. I had my earpiece out for a few minutes between setups.

Someone walked by and said, "Hey, Benjamin, I really appreciate your stance on life, man."

Mind you, this wasn't a political rally or a church event—it was a Georgia-Michigan game. (Georgia won, by the way—go Dawgs!) And the thing is, I get comments like this quite often.

A few months ago, a woman who works in Silicon Valley messaged me to say how much she appreciated my speaking out for life because she couldn't. "I can't even retweet or repost anything about this," she said, "or I could get into trouble."

Unsolicited comments like these are encouraging to me, because there are a lot of people out there who, for one reason or another, are unable to speak out on issues that are important to them. So if I can use my platform to advocate on their behalf, you'd better believe I'm going to do it.

That said, I get why people might question my involvement. For what it's worth, this wasn't part of my original game plan either.

A MATTER OF BLACK AND WHITE

When I was a kid, all I wanted was to be a football player and a missionary. And an astronaut. And president of the United States. But a pro-life activist? It never even crossed my mind.

As the oldest of six kids, I grew up in a home that was

unquestionably pro-life, though I don't remember that exact terminology being used. What I do remember was my parents making this message abundantly clear: "You care for other people because all people are valuable in the eyes of God."

My father was a parole officer and later a pastor, and with eight of us under one roof, every dollar was taken into account. Yet my parents always had an open-door policy, welcoming others in, giving faithfully, and serving as counselors and leaders in our community and church family.

For most of my childhood, we lived in all-Black neighborhoods and were members of predominantly Black churches. But in my early years I attended a white Christian school, and we would visit an all-white church on occasion. So from as far back as I can remember, I was aware of the economic disparity between Black and white.

This disparity was on full display every morning as we drove to school. To earn income for our tuition, my mother drove the school bus. Because she had to pick up kids from all over the city, we drove through every type of neighborhood you can imagine—wealthy, middle class, and impoverished; some all-Black and some all-white.

I remember one neighborhood in particular called Ghent. It was in a very well-to-do area of Norfolk, Virginia, with a lot of expensive homes, and it was almost exclusively white. Over time I learned that Ghent used to be all Black, but the city stopped taking care of the roads, sidewalks, and sewers until it fell into a state of disrepair. All the Black families were forced out through eminent domain, the old houses were bulldozed, and larger, more expensive homes were built—ones that only affluent white people could afford.

Every day as we wound our way through town, I would look out the school bus windows at the Black neighborhoods, which were tired, dilapidated, and worn. Then I'd see the newer, cleaner, decidedly nicer white neighborhoods like Ghent, and I struggled to make sense of it. I knew that not every job paid the same, but still . . .

I saw how hard my parents and neighbors worked. So why did we live in such different places? It just didn't make sense. Nor did it seem fair. If we were all, as my parents had always impressed upon us, equally valuable in the eyes of God, why did some people seem worse off than others for no reason I could discern other than the color of their skin?

Then, when I was ten, I watched Rodney King get savagely beaten by four white police officers on TV. That, more than anything, entrenched in me the reality that there are two markedly different worlds out there.

By the time I was sixteen, I was keenly aware that as a Black person, who you are and how you look can be a problem simply by virtue of caste.

I remember my dad sitting me down and earnestly telling me, "Benjamin, policemen have a tough job to do, and you never know what kind of day they've already had. So if a police officer pulls you over, don't make any sudden movements. Show them your hands and be respectful, because you might not get the same grace somebody else would."

Daddy's experience as a parole officer aside, I'd seen enough lack of parity between Black and white by that point to know he was right.

Prolific author and sociologist W. E. B. Du Bois talks about what he calls the "double-consciousness" of Black America:

feeling fully American but at the same time not, and seeing yourself not only from your own perspective but also in the way others perceive you.

"It is a peculiar sensation," he said, "this double-consciousness, this sense of always looking at one's self through the eyes of others, of measuring one's soul by the tape of a world that looks on in amused contempt and pity. One ever feels his two-ness—an American, a Negro; two souls, two thoughts, two unreconciled strivings; two warring ideals in one dark body, whose dogged strength alone keeps it from being torn asunder."[6]

Blackness is beautiful, but realizing you are a member of the "other" brings both pride and precaution. You are forced to reckon with the perception that white America, as the majority culture, may have of your ilk. You try to maintain a sense of dignity, strength, and pride, all the while grappling with what feels like visitation rights in the land of your birth.

One summer, my father took our family to visit some of the old Civil War battlefields. Daddy was a history buff, and I vividly remember a framed painting that hung on our living room wall depicting one of those battles. It often captured my gaze, and I would imagine the invisible heaviness each man in the scene must have carried alongside his bayonet.

The fighting men in blue and gray were engaged in the bloody fury and confusion of combat, yet glory rose from the carnage and death. For the 54th Massachusetts (the first Black regiment organized in the North), it was a willing exchange to lay down one's life on the sands of Morris Island, South Carolina, to secure freedom for themselves and their descendants.

That summer, as my family walked the grounds where blood was shed to help free the enslaved, I felt an increasing sense of affirmation that no matter what I eventually became—a football player, a missionary, or even an astronaut—I would fight for the oppressed, the outcast, and the voiceless. In short, I wanted to be an abolitionist.

So really, my involvement in the pro-life movement started with a passion for justice.

Then came Grace.

THE GIFT OF GRACE

I remember it like it was yesterday.

It was the winter of 2008, the middle of my fifth season with the Patriots. Kirsten and I had been married for three years, and she was seven months pregnant with our first child.

We had taken advantage of a bye week to spend some time with my parents in Rock Hill, South Carolina. As it happened, a friend of Kirsten's who lived just half an hour away, in Charlotte, had her own 3D/4D ultrasound business as a service and outreach to expectant mothers in the area. She asked if we would be interested in getting a scan.

We'd already had a regular ultrasound, so it wasn't necessary, but as first-time parents, we couldn't resist getting a sneak peek. Besides, it's never too early to get a jump on that baby album.

We had a name picked out already. Well . . . Kirsten did. As soon as we found out we were having a girl, we went back and forth and nearly chose another name. But one day while she was listening to a new rendition of "Amazing Grace" (she never was a fan of the slow version), Kirsten felt in her spirit, *Her name is Grace.*

Personally, I thought it sounded like an old lady's name, but Kirsten was certain. The more I considered it, the more I began to love it as well. Ephesians 2:8 says, "By grace you have been saved, through faith—and this is not from yourselves, it is the gift of God" (NIV).

A gift from God. It's hard to argue with that.

When we got to the office, Kirsten's friend ushered us into a welcoming little room with a sofa, a comfortable chair for me to sit in, warm lighting, and soft music playing in the background. It was a totally different experience from when we got our eighteen-week ultrasound, which was in a more clinical setting. At that appointment, the focus was on taking measurements and checking vitals. This, however, was an *experience.*

I sat next to Kirsten, holding her hand, while we waited for the first images to appear on the screen in front of us. Honestly, I wasn't sure what to expect. Our first ultrasound had looked like a staticky black-and-white blur that the sonographer had to interpret for us. How she was able to discern arms and legs amid all the pulsating shadows, I have no idea.

At first all we could make out was a large sepia-colored mass.

"That's the back," our friend said, adjusting the screen slightly. "Let's see if we can't get this little one to turn around." She began gently pressing on Kirsten's stomach, and we both watched the screen as her hands deftly rotated the mass, little by little.

Then, all at once, we saw our daughter's face. She looked almost as though she were made of clay, but I could clearly make out every facial feature, as crisp and clear as if I were holding her in my arms.

Kirsten and I couldn't speak. We just stared at the screen with tears in our eyes as our little gift from God rocked back and forth, her legs flexing, her tiny fists clenching and unclenching.

It's difficult to describe—that feeling of seeing your child for the first time. Is it wonder? Is it joy? Is it awe? The answer is yes.

I was already excited about starting a family. I had even gotten over the fact that our baby wasn't a boy (four of them coming soon enough). But watching this extraordinary little being moving in the womb felt at once exhilarating and terrifying.

As the oldest of six, I can remember at least four of my siblings coming home from the hospital. And of course, I'd helped a little with feedings and changings, so it wasn't as if babies were foreign to me. But staring into the face of your own child? There simply aren't words to describe it.

Then she yawned.

And so did I.

"Did you see that?" I asked, laughing through my tears. "Grace just yawned, and I yawned right back! How crazy is that?"

There was no question about it: this wasn't just a collection of cells or a hazy shadow fluttering on a screen. This was a real live human being. This was our daughter. This was Grace.

As we walked back to our car that afternoon, Kirsten smiled at me. "Wow, I just got to see my daughter before I get to hold my daughter." Then she said, "Baby, I want to find a way to provide this for other women. Every mom should be able to have this experience."

I knew exactly how she felt. When you have an experience like that, you want to share it with everyone, and you don't want money or accessibility to be an obstacle.

Beyond desire, though, we had no idea how to move forward. Kirsten's friend had purchased her own equipment and was renting out the office space. But getting the equipment solved only part of the problem. Because 3D ultrasounds are an elective procedure, they aren't covered by insurance. And they're expensive.

Kirsten was right. Being able to see your preborn child and form an emotional bond with them shouldn't be a privilege reserved for people of a certain financial standing who have access to a private provider. It should be a viable option for everyone. The question was, *How?*

LIFE FINDS A WAY

In 2016—eight years, four more kids, three seasons with the Browns, and three seasons with the Saints later—I found myself in Baltimore playing for the Ravens. I had just written a book called *Under Our Skin*, about racial injustice in America, and I'd been asked to do an interview with a pregnancy resource center that wanted to hear my thoughts on how race factors into the abortion discussion.

To be honest, I hadn't spent an extensive amount of time

examining the history of abortion. But I had done research on the impact of racial injustice, and it was difficult to ignore the link between the two. I knew, for example, that compared to other ethnic groups, abortion disproportionately reduces the Black population, that the American eugenics movement was the ground from which the abortion industry blossomed, and that abortion access hadn't solved any of the socioeconomic issues Black people continue to face. The research I'd done indicated that groups like Planned Parenthood intentionally promote abortion to minorities.

I knew from both inquiry and observation that the odds are inordinately stacked against Black women, and even though the notion of deliberately terminating a pregnancy runs counter to everything I believe, I'm sympathetic to what many of these women are facing. Regardless of a person's skin color, the decision to willfully terminate the life of your own child is an unthinkably difficult and painful one to have to make, and I would never be so bold as to presume that women in this position are having abortions flippantly.

I shared these thoughts in the interview, adding that Kirsten and I were thinking about different ways we could use our foundation to support the pro-life cause.[7]

The next thing I knew, the article had gone viral. It was picked up by MSN, BET, CBN, Fox News, Sporting News, the *Christian Post*, the *Drudge Report*, the *Washington Times*, and *Christian Today*. As it turns out, when you're Black and in the NFL, and you start talking about abortion, people tend to take notice.

Shortly after this interview, I received an email from Jeanne Mancini, the president of March for Life, asking if I would speak at the upcoming March for Life event in Washington, DC.

I had never even heard of the March for Life, but I didn't hesitate to accept. How could I say no? Not only had I just made an open offer in the interview, but for the past eight years, Kirsten and I had been seeking opportunities to advocate for justice and serve marginalized men, women, and children in the US and around the world. Our foundation had been created specifically to bring the hope and love of Jesus Christ to those who need it most—first and foremost by meeting their physical needs. What greater physical need is there than to simply be allowed to live?

Believe me when I say that I had no idea how big the March for Life was. When I arrived, I was shocked to discover there were thousands of people gathered on the National Mall that day. And it wasn't just women. There were countless men, too, plus buses full of teenagers and young kids who had come from all over the country.

With all the people cheering and holding up signs, the event almost had a pep rally feel. I have to admit, that threw me a little. I'd expected the tone to be more solemn. After all, we were talking about the loss of more than 60 million pre-born children. And while there were small pockets of people gathered in prayer and tearstained faces dotting the crowd, there was still an undeniable feeling of hope.

There's power that comes from knowing you're not alone—that there are other people out there fighting alongside you—fighting *for* you. It's a reminder that you're not by yourself. And when you're united together, you're capable of more than you could ever accomplish on your own.

I'd experienced a similar feeling many times during my NFL career, but this was altogether different. This wasn't just a game. This was literally a matter of life and death.

I began my speech by quoting one of my favorite Scripture passages, Jeremiah 9:23-24 (NASB): "Thus says the LORD, 'Let not a wise man boast of his wisdom, and let not the mighty man boast of his might, let not a rich man boast of his riches; but let him who boasts boast of this, that he understands and knows Me, that I am the LORD who exercises lovingkindness, justice and righteousness on the earth; for I delight in these things.'"

I encouraged everyone to remember the power of loving-kindness and to empathize with the men and women who had made the decision to terminate their pregnancies, regardless of whether they'd done so willingly or under duress. I expressed my hope that pro-life be not only a political stance but a way of life, encompassing the victims of sex trafficking and abuse, the hungry and the poor, the disadvantaged as well as the elite. I reminded them of our biblical commitment to justice—that those who take innocent life be held accountable, that lives never be forgotten under the guise of choice, and that we stay the course on days when the fire inside us burns, as well as on days when the ember flickers. I acknowledged that while this battle may seem never-ending, the end goal is more than worth the effort.

Finally, I issued a special call to the men in the crowd—and there were many. I told them that it was past time for us to be the leaders, caretakers, and providers we were meant to

be. That we as men must stand up for the lives of the innocent and their mothers in crisis. And that as important as
women have been in championing this cause, we men must
rise up and lead the charge. We must be silent no more.[8]

After that event, the floodgates opened. I started receiving speaking opportunities from other pro-life organizations,
pregnancy resource centers, fundraisers, and dozens of other
events.

That's when Kirsten finally got her wish.

SEEING IS BELIEVING

In 2018, I was invited to speak at the third annual Evangelicals
for Life Conference in Washington, DC. The event was
sponsored by Focus on the Family and the Southern Baptist
Convention's Ethics and Religious Liberty Commission
(ERLC), and as providence would have it, the topic of one
of the presentations that night was a partnership between
Focus on the Family's Option Ultrasound Program and
ERLC's Psalm 139 Project, both of which support expectant
moms by placing 3D/4D ultrasound machines in pregnancy
resource centers.

Kirsten was there with me, and as soon as the presentation
ended, we looked at each other and said, "We're doing this!"

Several months later, we donated our first 3D/4D ultrasound machine to the Severna Park Pregnancy Clinic just
outside Baltimore, in one of the country's most abortion-
friendly states.[9]

When Kirsten and I toured the facility, we learned that the
building's previous tenant was, of all things, an abortion clinic.

"When we walked [in], we found they had left overnight," the CEO of the clinic explained. "There were still bloody sponges on the floor, bloodstains on the floor, client files they had left behind. They didn't close; they simply moved to a very discreet location where they wouldn't have people out front protesting and holding signs and praying."[10]

She also told us that because the old clinic never changed the contact info on their website, they still received thousands of calls every year from women wanting to know how much an abortion would cost. Think about the gracious irony in that: calling to arrange for an abortion and finding a pro-life organization on the other end! I love when God does things like that.

The final stop on our tour was the prayer room. I was picturing a warm, welcoming space with pictures on the walls, lush carpeting, comfortable chairs, a coffee table, some bookshelves, and maybe even a sofa where people could come to reflect and pray in peace. Instead, we were ushered into a large, open room with a dingy tile floor and a handful of wooden chairs lining stark white walls. The only splash of color was a rectangular Persian throw rug, much too small for the room, sitting curiously off-center.

On closer inspection, I noticed that the walls were covered with handwritten notes—Scripture passages, in fact. As Kirsten and I made our way around the room, reading the hand-scribbled verses, our guide shared that the room we were standing in had once been the scene of countless late-term abortions. She lifted the edge of the Persian rug, revealing a faded yet unmistakable bloodstain on the tile, a somber reminder of what had once taken place within these stark walls. This room had purposely been left "as is" as a remembrance of "what once was."

When the battle becomes too much to bear, the staff comes to this space to pray, mourn, read, and recharge, surrounded by walls that once witnessed unrelenting death but now behold words of abundant life.

Since then, Kirsten and I have placed three more ultrasound machines in pregnancy clinics in cities we've lived in during my NFL career, in addition to my hometown. And though I don't have quantifiable statistics, we have learned through our various partners that many women who come to pregnancy centers considering an abortion experience a change of heart after seeing their child in vivid detail on the screen. For them, seeing truly is believing.

MAN ON A MISSION

Shortly after I retired from the NFL (the first time) in January 2019, the state of New York passed the Reproductive Health Act, essentially extending abortion rights up until birth. This news sent shock waves throughout the entire country.

Prior to the bill's passage into law, abortion was legal only during the first twenty-four weeks of pregnancy, after which a woman could get an abortion only if her life was at risk. Under the new law, a woman could get an abortion after twenty-four weeks—not just if her life was threatened but also if carrying the child to term was deemed detrimental to her health. The law also decriminalized abortion, eliminating the threat of prosecution for medical professionals who perform abortions. Further, it opened the door for nurse practitioners, physician assistants, and licensed midwives to perform abortions.[11]

Illinois quickly adopted similar laws, with Governor J. B. Pritzker vowing to make Illinois the most "abortion-friendly" state in the nation.[12] Since then, other states have followed suit.

With things heating up in the legislature and an election year around the corner, I was anxious to take a more active role in advocating for the preborn. I kept asking the Lord, "What else can I do? How can I help?"

A few weeks later, I got a call from a movie producer named Chad Bonham. I'd met Chad a few years earlier when he was working on a project highlighting Christian athletes, and we'd kept in touch ever since. Now he was working on a documentary about the impact of abortion on America. He'd seen some of the press Kirsten and I had been receiving for the ultrasound donations and wanted to know if I would be interested in getting involved. Needless to say, I was.

I spent the next several months talking with politicians, physicians, lawyers, advocates, and activists on both sides of the issue to paint a comprehensive picture of where the US stood on abortion. I discovered that the topic is far more layered and complex than many people realize. There are a multitude of factors—relational, economic, educational, political, and religious—that affect the way people feel about abortion, and the vast majority of people fall somewhere between the extremes. Yet we have a tendency to zero in on the most polarized ends of the spectrum, which ends up demonizing the other side, shutting down dialogue, and pushing us even further apart.

Our goal with the documentary was to model a civil discourse—to show the humanity behind the headlines and to model empathy. Whether or not we agree with someone's position, they are God's image bearers and deserving of dignity and respect, just like we are.

That's what it's been about from the beginning for me: valuing and protecting life—*all* life.

FOR SUCH A TIME AS THIS

When we look at Scripture, we tend to think that Moses always knew he was going to get people out of Egypt or that Peter had a pretty good idea from the beginning that he'd be called to spread the gospel. In actuality, however, God chose specific moments for specific people to speak and act on his behalf. The rest of the time they were off doing their own thing. That's what happened to me: I was going along, playing football, raising a family, and serving our local community as best I could. And then . . . *bam*!

If you'd told me when I was growing up that one day I'd be speaking at a March for Life rally in Washington, DC, donating ultrasound machines to pregnancy clinics, filming a documentary about abortion, or writing a book on how to make abortion unthinkable and unnecessary in a post-*Roe* world, I would have laughed and said, "Nah, not me, man. I'm gonna play in the NFL." The thought that I might do both never even occurred to me.

I've often said that God doesn't need football, but he can use it. I truly believe that God has put me in this particular space at this particular moment for a particular reason.

I don't know when this season will end, but I do know that for now, this is what he wants me to do, and I intend to be faithful to that call.

So now you know why I'm here. And no matter what has brought you here, and no matter where you stand in the pro-life/pro-choice conversation, my hope is that this book will be just that: a conversation. One about justice, dignity, empathy, taking responsibility, and coming together to make a positive impact in the lives of others.

Shortly before I began working on the documentary, Kirsten and I welcomed twin boys into our family. One day I came home from filming to find a young woman sitting in our living room. Her name was Nikki, and she was Kirsten's nurse practitioner and lactation consultant. After Kirsten introduced us, we spent some time talking, and before I knew it, I'd asked her to take part in the documentary.

As a Black woman, she understood the myriad issues that have plagued Black people for centuries and have made Black women particularly vulnerable to abortion. As a health-care worker, she was in the fight. She wasn't sitting in an ivory tower or drafting legislation. She was right there in the midst of it, working with pregnant women, watching them make decisions, and helping them take care of their babies. She loved life and wanted people to parent, but she also understood the very real, complicated reasons that drive some women to have an abortion.

When she sat down to talk with me on camera, I asked her how she felt we could best come together and have this conversation. She looked at me, smiled, and said, "First, we need to calm down. *Everybody* needs to calm down. And when I say 'calm down,' [I mean] putting down those extremes. Because if we come to the table not being open at all, we're going to be in our little lanes, and we're not going to want to try to understand what the other person is trying to say."[13]

She's right. As living beings, the issue of life is inherently important to us. That's why we become so emotionally charged whenever human flourishing is at stake, why we mourn when we lose loved ones, and why we're saddened whenever a tragedy occurs on our doorstep or around the world. However, if we hope to achieve any semblance of mutual understanding, we must engage one another with civility.

Now is not the time for extremism, for focusing on one side and one side alone. What we need is to come together in humility to honor, protect, and ensure the best possible life for both mother *and* child, not just for one or the other—or worse, one at the expense of the other. And we need to ensure the best possible life not just before birth but all the way to the tomb.

That's what it means to do justice.

That's why I take this issue so seriously.

And that's why I know that we still have a lot of work to do.

CHAPTER 2

A BRIEF HISTORY OF INJUSTICE

The way to right wrongs is to turn the light of truth upon them.

IDA B. WELLS

In 2019, I came out of a brief retirement to play one more season with the New England Patriots. That July, Kirsten—who had recently given birth to our twin boys—and I loaded all seven kids into our twelve-passenger van to make the trek from New Orleans to Boston. Along the way, we stopped in Montgomery, Alabama, to visit the National Memorial for Peace and Justice.

The memorial, a passion project of Bryan Stevenson (the attorney whose story is depicted in the book and film *Just Mercy*), honors the more than four thousand victims of racial terror lynchings throughout the South between 1877 and 1950.[1]

Not the typical family vacation, granted, but whenever

possible, Kirsten and I like to give our kids a sprinkling of American history they may not get in school. In *How the Word Is Passed*, Clint Smith writes, "There is enormous value in providing young people with the language, the history, and the framework to identify why their society looks the way it does."[2] I couldn't agree more.

Kirsten and I want our kids to grow into adults who understand not only the cultural context around them but also how it came to be, so we look for opportunities to personalize history and bring it to life. When I was playing with the Saints in 2015, instead of flying home with the team after our final regular-season game against the Falcons, Kirsten and I drove the kids to visit the National Voting Rights Museum and Institute in Selma, Alabama. In 2018, I took our two oldest girls, Grace and Naomi, on a civil rights pilgrimage from Montgomery to Selma, led by former congressman and civil rights activist John Lewis. The trip culminated in a march from Brown Chapel AME Church across the Edmund Pettus Bridge.

All that to say, the older kids were used to this sort of thing. Still, given the sensitive and potentially graphic nature of the Montgomery memorial, we thought it would be wise to prep the younger ones a bit first. The conversation went about as expected.

"What's lynching?" Isaiah, our seven-year-old, asked from the back seat.

"It's when people are killed," I explained, "usually by hanging. And it happened to 'brown' people a lot after the Civil War. Even though slavery was over, a lot of people were still mistreated, some in terrible ways, so this memorial was built to honor them."

"I thought we were going to Mimi's house," our youngest daughter, Eden, piped up.

"We are, baby," I assured her. "The memorial is on the way to Mimi's house. We're going to stop for about an hour."

"Why?" she pressed.

It's not easy competing with whatever surprise Kirsten's mom had waiting for them in Atlanta.

"Because, baby—" I caught her eye in the rearview mirror—"it's important that we understand our history."

Still, even I wasn't prepared for what we saw that day.

The memorial is massive. It consists of 805 rust-colored steel columns, roughly the size and shape of coffins, that are suspended from an expansive, flat roof. Each column is etched with the name of a victim, the date of their death, and the county and state where the lynching occurred.

When you first approach the monument, it's at eye level, but as you walk through, the floor slopes downward until eventually the columns are all hanging above you, like actual lynching victims. The surrounding walls are adorned with engraved silver plaques that bear brief epitaphs of the men, women, and children whose lives were mercilessly snuffed out.

Jim Eastman, lynched in Brunswick, Tennessee, in 1887 for not allowing a white man to beat him in a fight

Warren Powell, 14, lynched in East Point, Georgia, in 1889 for "frightening" a white girl

Mary Turner, 1918, hung upside down, burned, and
then sliced open so that her unborn child fell to the
ground after denouncing her husband's lynching by
a rampaging white mob

Jesse Thornton, lynched in Luverne, Alabama, in
1940 for addressing a white police officer without
the title "mister"

It's incredibly powerful. It's also incredibly somber.

Just outside the memorial is a life-size sculpture of six
enslaved African men and women in rusty shackles and
chains, struggling to break free. One is a mother holding an
infant, their faces strained with anguish. Grace and Naomi
were particularly stricken by this depiction. I was too. The
sculpture's proximity to the memorial served as a metaphor
for the multiple layers of injustice that have been heaped on
generations of people.

"Wow," I quietly remarked to Kirsten, "imagine finally
breaking free from the chains of slavery, only to fall victim
to lynch mobs . . ."

As hard as it is to believe, there were once laws legislat-
ing that crimes committed against a Black person by a white
person were not crimes at all.[3] But as we walked along the
memorial grounds, the unthinkable started to feel downright
palpable.

It's hard to say how much of that experience our kids
grasped or will ultimately remember. The day was hot and
muggy, the drive there had been long, and their grandmother's
embrace was beckoning. It was a lot to take in—especially

at their ages. But for me, it was a sobering reminder that for Black people in this land, personhood and legal protection have been the exception, not the norm.

RECONSTRUCTING JUSTICE

The Reverend Jesse Jackson wrote, "If something can be dehumanized through the rhetoric used to describe it, then the major battle has been won. . . . That is why the Constitution called us three-fifths human and then whites further dehumanized us by calling us 'niggers.' It was part of the dehumanizing process. The first step was to distort the image of us as human beings in order to justify that which they wanted to do and not even feel like they had done anything wrong."[4]

Congress attempted to correct this egregious crime against humanity after the Civil War ended by passing the thirteenth, fourteenth, and fifteenth amendments—formally abolishing slavery and granting freedmen equal protection under the law and the right to vote. Prior to 1865, Black men had been able to vote in only a handful of Northern states, and practically none held political office. During this period of Reconstruction, however, Black political power expanded. From the halls of Congress to the chambers of state and local legislature, nearly two thousand Black men took public office, sixteen of whom assumed their rightful seats in Congress across the table from former enslavers.[5]

Reconstruction also created an incubator of economic and educational advancement. Missionaries and churches opened schools for former slaves, and literacy increased.

Many of them went from working the land to owning their own parcel of it. This period of advancement was short-lived, however, especially in the Southern states.

All across the South, landowners who resented the loss of free labor and legislators who feared a shift in power, especially in states like South Carolina where Black citizens vastly outnumbered white citizens, implemented "Black Codes." These laws severely restricted the behavior of Black people to ensure their continued availability as cheap labor and to prevent them from advancing in social status.

Strict vagrancy laws were passed, and those caught congregating at night or without written proof of employment risked brutal beatings and arrest. State militias colluded with landowners, leasing convicted Black men as slave labor. Meanwhile, racially motivated hate groups, most notably the Ku Klux Klan, were formed, intent on maintaining white supremacy through acts of calculated violence and terror.

The Black Codes were followed by the equally oppressive Jim Crow laws, which legalized racial segregation and further marginalized the formerly enslaved and their progeny. Several states instituted literacy requirements, poll taxes, and constitutional quizzes to prevent Blacks from registering to vote.[6] Others limited the amount and type of property Black people could own. And as with the Black Codes, those who defied the Jim Crow laws faced arrest, fines, beatings, and even death.[7]

It didn't stop there. At the end of World War II, President Roosevelt signed the G.I. Bill to help returning veterans pay for housing and education. But much like their post-Reconstruction-era ancestors, Black veterans faced innumerable obstacles to claiming their benefits. Blocked from receiving mortgage assistance, they were locked out of the postwar housing boom. And with segregation still in force throughout the North and the South, most were shut out of white colleges and universities, leaving a large portion of the Black population with neither a house to call their own nor a college degree. So while employment, education, and earning opportunities flourished for white veterans, the wealth accumulation that would have brought some semblance of economic equality was stunted by redlining and restrictive covenants.

Despite Congress's promise of "'one measure of justice' for all persons, regardless of race,"[8] Black people struggled for decades to assimilate into a fearful and prejudiced society—one that was unwilling to deviate from the status quo, one that was equal in word only.

This racial wealth gap continues to be a key indicator of a lack of equality. While there have been periods of increased convergence since emancipation—notably the civil rights era, from 1960 through the 1970s[9]—the racial wealth gap has, in fact, slowly widened in my lifetime.

I remember reading a shocking report from Boston, a city we called home for seven years, which stated that the median net worth for white households in the area was nearly a quarter of a million dollars, but for Black nonimmigrant families, it was just eight dollars.[10] Across the nation, white families have a median net worth of $171,000, compared to $17,000 for their average Black counterparts.[11]

In spite of contemporary efforts to pursue income equality, the cumulative impact of discriminatory policy, programs, and practices over generations dwarfs the positive effect of these necessary attempts to address it. The essence of this wealth gap is not solely that the enslaved and their descendants have been excluded from opportunity but that individuals and institutions over the course of our nation's history have incessantly exploited them for economic gain.

When I look back at that time of Civil War Reconstruction, I often think, *You know what . . . if America had truly been committed to justice at that point and done everything it could to establish equality—not just by passing amendments but by repenting of its abhorrent actions, restoring the human rights it systematically stripped, and providing redress for Black people so they could be fully and completely assimilated into American society—we wouldn't be dealing with a lot of the problems the Black community is dealing with right now.*

As things stand, we are still experiencing the impact of Black Codes and convict leasing. Ironically, when the enslaved grasped freedom, reparations were given, but not to those who had been wrongfully denied restitution for their labor. Instead, reparations were given to some slave owners to make up for lost labor and lost property in the wake of emancipation.

This is the problem when "we the people" attempt to define and dispense justice from a limited, human perspective. We all say we want people to be treated equally, but when we have different ideas of what justice looks like, it's impossible to have one equal measure. Case in point: both those who wrote the thirteenth, fourteenth, and fifteenth amendments, and those who stripped away those rights, subjugating people they deemed inferior, believed they were doing justice. Likewise, if you were to speak to members of both the pro-life and pro-choice camps—and I have—they would ardently declare that they are fighting for justice.

The problem, then, lies not in our desire for justice but rather in our definition of it.

HALF MEASURES

Justice is a word that sometimes lacks concrete definition. Yet countless groups, from supporters of apartheid to Amnesty International, have claimed it as their rallying cry.

Most dictionary definitions of justice center on the idea of treating conflicting claims with impartiality or assigning merited rewards and punishments. Some definitions imply alignment with what is morally upright and correct, while others take a more purist approach, focusing on the root word—*just*—meaning "legally correct."

The problem with human definitions, however, is that they are subject to human amendments. Collective agreement determines the parameters of justice, and those who venture outside those boundaries are subject to public reprimand. In other words, the majority rules.

If humankind has the final authority, our generation has no more right to condemn our ancestors for their handling of social issues than they have to criticize our current legislative decisions. Without absolutes, there is no foundation for cogent arguments that produce substantive change. Historical context and personal predilections move the slide rule one way, then another, with everyone simply doing what seems right in their own eyes (see Judges 21:25).

Of course, when humanity is allowed to determine what justice is, it is also allowed to determine who is a worthy recipient. Even the most cursory review of world history reveals that, whether intentionally or unintentionally, those in positions of power routinely secure and maintain their social and economic advantages at the expense of others. While some civilizations brazenly conquer and subjugate, others espouse ideologies of equality but fail to practice what they preach. Either way, the result is the same. Justice is defined and determined by those in positions of privilege and dispensed on those deemed worthy, often in careful doses, lest it upset the balance of power.

What happened during the Civil War Reconstruction era is a perfect example. The failure of our country's leaders to assimilate the formerly enslaved into American society lay not in the verbiage of their amendments but in their execution of them. While outlawing oppression is necessary, it does not, in and of itself, guarantee human thriving. Conceived only as a way to erase an unsightly stain on our country's conscience, the government's efforts at emancipation were never fully committed to flourishing. They were, at best, half measures. And half measures do not suffice.

The only way we can achieve one true measure of justice is to foster a culture that genuinely values *every* human life and is committed not only to protecting human life but to creating an environment where life can be lived fully and abundantly. And to do that, we need to look not to legislature but to God's Word.

ONE TRUE MEASURE

True justice exists outside of human jurisdiction; it begins and ends with God. In fact, the very idea of justice emanates from God's character. Since he is the very essence of justice, he defines it and sets the standard for it.

Deuteronomy 32:4 says:

He is the Rock; his deeds are perfect.
　　Everything he does is just and fair.
He is a faithful God who does no wrong;
　　how just and upright he is!

Likewise, Psalm 89:14 says, "Righteousness and justice are the foundation of [his] throne. Unfailing love and truth walk before [him] as attendants."

God determined and dispensed the first measure of justice in the Garden long before the United States ratified the Constitution. He levied consequences on Adam and Eve for their willful disobedience, and though his administration of justice was swift and severe, he did not stop at humankind's expulsion from Paradise. Because of his unfailing love for humanity, he went to great lengths to ensure our eventual return to him through the atoning, just sacrifice of his Son, Jesus Christ.

God does not work in half measures. He reconciles completely.

In his book *Generous Justice*, Tim Keller says that all through Scripture, God advocates for those with the least earthly protection and advantage. That's what it means to do justice.[12]

Time and again, the Bible instructs us to take care of "the least of these," especially brothers and sisters in Christ (Matthew 25:45). Isaiah 1:17 gives us this challenge: "Do good. Seek justice. Help the oppressed. Defend the cause of orphans, [and] fight for the rights of widows." Likewise, Luke 14:12-14 says, "When you give a dinner or a banquet, do not invite your friends or your brothers or your relatives or rich neighbors. . . . When you give a feast, invite the poor, the crippled, the lame, the blind, and you will be blessed" (ESV).

Luke 4 records Jesus entering the synagogue in his hometown of Nazareth, where he read from the scroll of the prophet Isaiah, fulfilling prophecies written some seven hundred years earlier:

> The Spirit of the LORD is upon me,
>   for he has anointed me to bring Good News
>   to the poor.
> He has sent me to proclaim that captives will be
>   released,
>   that the blind will see,
>   that the oppressed will be set free,
>   and that the time of the LORD's favor has come.
> LUKE 4:18-19

Jesus' mission and ministry embodied every prophetic word he claimed that day. Through parables, sermons, and miracles, Jesus mercifully addressed both the spiritual and the physical needs of those who sought him. He exhorted his followers to be distinguishable from the world, doing good works that bring glory to God and benefit people (see Matthew 5:16).

He spent three years ministering to the broken and the vulnerable, all the while chastising and condemning the elite of the day for abusing their power. Then, like a sheep led to the slaughter, he endured an unfair trial and crucifixion. At that dark moment, he may have seemed helpless by human standards, but that's because his authority and agenda are of an entirely different dimension.

Our hope for justice is in his power. Our mandate for justice is in his words. Our understanding of justice is in his sacrifice. And our assurance of justice is in his promise:

> Blessed are the poor in spirit,
>   for theirs is the kingdom of heaven.
> Blessed are those who mourn,
>   for they will be comforted.
> Blessed are the meek,
>   for they will inherit the earth.
> Blessed are those who hunger and thirst for righteousness,
>   for they will be filled.
> Blessed are the merciful,
>   for they will be shown mercy.
> Blessed are the pure in heart,
>   for they will see God.
> Blessed are the peacemakers,
>   for they will be called children of God.
> Blessed are those who are persecuted because of
>   righteousness,
>   for theirs is the kingdom of heaven.

Blessed are you when people insult you, persecute
you and falsely say all kinds of evil against you
because of me. Rejoice and be glad, because great
is your reward in heaven.

MATTHEW 5:3-12, NIV

Jesus' return will usher in a Kingdom where fairness and
impartiality will prevail. He came to proclaim justice to the
nations (see Matthew 12:18), and he will not grow weak
or become discouraged until justice reigns on the earth (see
Isaiah 42:1-4).

The resurrection of Christ provides hope for a world
riddled with pain, inequity, destruction, and death. But this
hope in what will be does not absolve us of our responsibility
to do justice now.

SOCIAL JUSTICE

As believers, we cannot turn a blind eye when people
are suffering, especially when we have resources to help.
Vulnerability comes in many different forms, including the
impoverished, the outcast, the abused, the sick, the lonely,
and the abandoned. And we are called to address all of them.

For years now, Kirsten and I have been involved with
the International Justice Mission (IJM). Founded by a small
group of human rights attorneys, IJM seeks to protect people
in poverty from violence, human trafficking, and abuse of
power—both in the United States and around the globe.[13]

What makes this organization different from a lot of
other relief agencies is that their goal is not just to rescue

victims but to disrupt and apprehend the perpetrators and strengthen the existing justice systems. They want to stop these crimes against humanity from happening in the first place. In other words, they're not just fighting injustice; they're putting systems in place to *eradicate* it.

In 2017, Kirsten and I led a group of friends and teammates on a trip with IJM to the Dominican Republic field office to support their work combating the sex trafficking of minors. Currently there are an estimated 1.7 million children in the global commercial sex trade.[14]

While we were there, we had the opportunity to meet with some of the kids who had been rescued and were recovering in IJM's aftercare program. They were between the ages of four and fourteen, many of them young girls who had been exploited—in some cases by their own family members.

The kids all spoke Spanish and I don't, but we were able to connect by playing games and tossing a football around together. At one point, we played a game where each of us adults had a little note card stuck to our foreheads with a word like *farmer* or *firefighter* written in Spanish. We teamed up with the kids while they acted out the word and we guessed it.

I was matched with a little girl who couldn't have been more than six years old. She was a tiny thing who barely came up to my waist. I knelt down and said hello, and she surprised me by understanding and responding with a little English. She told me her name was Sophia. After we played the game, I gave her a little hug, and she went on her way.

As the IJM team began walking us through our agenda for the day, I started crying uncontrollably. I was so overwhelmed with grief for this little girl who had been victimized by a member of her own family—someone who was supposed to protect her, someone she was supposed to be able to trust. This person took advantage of her innocence and wounded her deeply, quite possibly irreparably. As the father of three young girls myself, I found it too much to bear.

This little girl deserved so much better. She deserved love. She deserved justice.

The Hebrew word for justice is *mishpat*, which basically means that every person who commits a crime is given the same punishment, regardless of age, gender, race, or social status. It also means that everyone is afforded equal care and protection.[15]

In Scripture, justice often appears in conjunction with righteousness. Most people equate the word *righteousness* with things like personal integrity, clean living, Bible reading, prayer, or daily devotions. But in the Bible, righteousness, or *tzadeqah*, refers to the way we are to conduct our daily relationships with family, friends, and our community— with fairness, generosity, and equity.

When these two words, *tzadeqah* and *mishpat*, are tied together (as they are more than three dozen times throughout Scripture), the English expression that best conveys their meaning is "social justice."

That's pretty fitting, especially when you consider that if we treated people the way they should be treated—with fairness, kindness, love, and generosity—then protecting the vulnerable and punishing wrongdoers wouldn't even be necessary. Simply put, if we treated each other with righteousness, there would be no need for justice.

When you think about it, isn't that what parents try to teach their kids? To treat others with kindness, civility, and respect?

With seven children in the Watson house, we have ample opportunity to model social justice. Whenever there's an infraction of some kind, my wife and I levy the appropriate punishment—and believe me when I say that nobody appreciates the idea of meting out "one measure of justice" like a parent with more than one child. But in addition to providing consequences, we also try to right the wrong and help the offending child take steps toward genuine reconciliation so a loving relationship can be restored. In other words, it's not just about mitigating an altercation; it's about instilling a sense of righteousness that renders the need for future justice obsolete.

After all, that's the ultimate goal, not just in playroom squabbles but in society at large: to honor and value every human life so fully and completely that we do right by our fellow humans not because we fear punitive justice but because we believe in and value *protective* justice.

THE BEST TEACHER

I took my kids to see the National Memorial for Peace and Justice because I wanted them to understand our history—where we came from, how we got here, and what we had to endure and overcome to get where we are today. I believe history is a great teacher. Too often, however, we assume superiority over the generations before us and think we're immune to their evil.

It's easy, for example, to condemn our nineteenth-century ancestors for injustices perpetrated against the marginalized and enslaved. It's much more difficult to identify and indict our contemporaries for discriminatory hiring practices, residential segregation, wage discrepancies, and racial disparities in sentencing. Too often we pretend that injustice occurred regularly in the past but rarely in the present. We hesitate to consider the latter, because doing so places us in the uncomfortable crosshairs of requisite action or intentional apathy. We must make a choice.

Likewise, it's convenient to claim that modern-day determinants of health and wealth have no roots in the social and political systems of the past. This is about as accurate as saying a 150-foot-tall oak tree is a product of this generation, when in reality the seed was planted long before we were born.

Modern-day redlining and gentrification, for example, are direct descendants of twentieth-century Jim Crow laws, as is unequal education for many Black children and the credit-lending habits of banks. It's also the reason pollution-spewing industrial plants are built in certain neighborhoods, while parks, recreational facilities, and grocery stores are established in others.[16]

This landscape has a direct impact on every aspect of life, including motherhood. Statistics show that Black women face maternal mortality rates nearly three times those of white women.[17] They are also less likely to have health insurance or access to prenatal care. In a country with an ever-widening wealth gap, roughly one-third of Black single mothers live under the poverty line.[18]

This is where things get uncomfortable for pro-life

advocates who recite the statistics but fail to take them to their logical conclusions. If Black women are four times more likely to have abortions than white women,[19] one can only conclude either that Black parents enjoy killing their children more than white parents (which is clearly not the case) or that multiple social, economic, and ideological factors have been compounding and intensifying since the mid-nineteenth century to create a crucible of susceptibility.

When we consider that the clear majority of women who experience problems after an abortion say they would have preferred to parent if their circumstances had been different,[20] and when we consider that data from reporting states indicates that roughly 40 percent of women seeking an abortion are Black,[21] it becomes clear that generations of compounded injustices are partly responsible for creating what feels like, for many women, an impossible environment in which to have and raise a child.

WHY GETTING IT RIGHT MATTERS

Embracing biblical justice allows us to return to the original blueprint when the world around us creates definitions of its own choosing. If justice were simply a legal notion derived in the mind, and if the law determined what is just, then any type of abuse could be condoned based on its legal status. That means that everything from chattel slavery to domestic abuse to sex trafficking to abortion would be sheltered by a canopy of justice until the ballot box or the Supreme Court determined otherwise.

Legal status will never guarantee true impartiality, because if the standard for justice is determined by human power and influence, it will always be subject to the whims of an ever-evolving culture. That's why new amendments are passed and old laws and rulings are overturned. Human-ordained justice is subjective, changing with the times, and often lacks parity. But true justice—as seen in Scripture—is ordained by God. That makes it unchanging, free from bias, and rooted in love.

If we rely too heavily on partisan legislature, social justice becomes more about a political stance than about protecting the vulnerable and eliminating obstacles to flourishing for mothers, fathers, and children. Voting pro-life may help protect the child in the womb, but it doesn't provide the assistance required for that child to flourish once born. Even when government-assisted programs are present, they can't help the child who isn't given the chance to live. Public policy has the potential to sustain life or to take it away. But true justice is not just about politics—it never will be.

Justice is bigger than politics because God is bigger than politics. This is not about whether we lean red or blue. This is about ensuring "one measure of justice" for people of different races, ethnicities, and socioeconomic backgrounds; for the preborn child; and for the child who has already been born—from the nursery to the nursing home.

Justice is about treating all people with kindness, fairness, and generosity, not because it has been legislated by Congress but because we have been commanded by God, the Creator of justice, to protect the weak and the vulnerable.

American culture likes to say that justice is blind, but justice has never been blind—at least not in a human context. That's why God continues to impress on people through his Word the importance of fighting for and administering justice.

Personally, I think justice should be blind, in that its purpose is to deliver punishment or protection to people equally, without favoritism or bias. But I also believe that justice has to be able to see who is being treated unjustly. Pursuing justice requires people to open their eyes to the many ways injustice has impacted people historically and to understand how past injustices continue to impact the descendants of those people today. It does no good for justice to be blind if we're unable to see where injustice has wreaked havoc and needs to be rectified.

As Langston Hughes wrote,

That Justice is a blind goddess
Is a thing to which we black are wise.
Her bandage hides two festering sores
That once perhaps were eyes.[22]

Simply put, if the United States truly desired to break its caste system, it should not have stopped at emancipation. Reparations should have been properly made, promises of equality fulfilled, opportunities for advancement ensured, and justice rightly defended.

Likewise, it is an incomplete work to stop at passing legal restrictions or banning abortion. The higher, more complete calling is to address the factors that drive abortion decisions. We can begin doing so by removing the obstacles of economic marginalization and oppression that have been in place since emancipation. Only then will justice truly be served and full reparations made.

History is a great teacher. Unfortunately, we have been poor students. But it's not too late—history doesn't have to repeat itself yet again. We are now entering a post-*Roe* Reconstruction era, and once again, we have the opportunity to right past wrongs and focus our energy on creating life-giving policies and practices to help families, neighbors, and churches walk alongside women facing unexpected pregnancies. We can focus on building stronger social safety nets, more robust economic opportunities, safer neighborhoods, and thriving spiritual communities where both mother and child can flourish.

In *The Color of Law*, Richard Rothstein writes,

> As citizens in this democracy, we—all of us, white, black, Hispanic, Asian, Native American, and others—bear a collective responsibility to enforce our Constitution and to rectify past violations whose effects endure. Few of us may be the direct descendants of those who perpetuated a segregated system or those who were its most exploited victims. African Americans cannot await rectification of past wrongs as a gift, and white Americans collectively do not owe it to African Americans to rectify them. We, all of us, owe this to ourselves. As American citizens, whatever routes we or our particular ancestors took to get to this point, we're all in this together now.[23]

We are all in this together. And it's going to take all of us working together to turn the tide, right a century of wrongs, and make choosing life a viable option for millions of abortion-determined women.

CHAPTER 3

A QUESTION OF HUMAN DIGNITY

The most disrespected person in America is the Black woman.
The most unprotected person in America is the Black woman.
The most neglected person in America is the Black woman.

MALCOLM X

Let's talk numbers for a minute. We know that a Black woman in the US is nearly four times more likely to have an abortion than a white woman.[1] Given that the Black population in the US currently stands somewhere around 44 million, abortion has effectively reduced the size of the Black community in this country by more than 30 percent. This does not include the children and grandchildren each member of the missing generation may have produced.[2]

Regardless of a person's opinion about abortion, the fact that it disproportionately eliminates members of a specific minority community represents a significant sociological problem. "Call this what you will," says theologian John Piper. "When the slaughter has a minority's face and the percentages are double that of the white community and the killers are almost all white, something is going on here that ought to make the lovers of racial equality and racial harmony wake up."[3]

Of course, recognizing that abortion disproportionately impacts Black women is one thing. Understanding why is another.

———————————

Last summer our family went on vacation to the Florida Panhandle. After a few days of relaxing in the sun and playing in the sand, we piled back into the family van and began the five-hour drive home to Atlanta. About an hour and a half from home, in Alabama, I steered off I-85 onto what quickly turned into an old country road. The kids were so engrossed in the movie they were watching that they didn't even ask where we were going until we were a good mile away from the interstate.

A few minutes later, we pulled into Moton Field, home of the Tuskegee Airmen National Historic Site.

We could see the heat rising off the pavement as we made the walk from the parking lot to the historic airstrip. This memorial was established to celebrate America's first Black military airmen, who served their country with unmatched courage and distinction during World War II.

While we were there, we got to hold a handmade parachute one of the seamstresses sewed for the pilots. Kirsten and I marveled at the precision required to take such an enormous piece of fabric and make it fit neatly into a bag no larger than a middle schooler's backpack—hiding in plain sight unless it had to be deployed.

After looking at some of the other artifacts and making sure the kids didn't climb all over the meticulously restored Red Tail P-51 Mustang aircraft, Kirsten and I loaded everyone back into the van and headed onto the highway. As we turned out of the parking lot, we passed the green and brown sign indicating the site's status as a National Park Foundation historical marker.

We pass similar signage on I-85 every time we drive through that area of Alabama, but I've never seen a sign commemorating the "Tuskegee experiment," an egregious example of human medical experimentation whose outcomes still reverberate today.

In this experiment conducted between 1932 and 1972 by the United States Public Health Service and the Centers for Disease Control and Prevention on a group of nearly six hundred sharecroppers, doctors recruited Black men, two-thirds with latent syphilis, promising them medical care and treatment but providing none, even though penicillin became readily available during the study. The men were even prevented from seeking treatment from local doctors that could have saved their lives. Instead, the medical team ruthlessly tracked the disease's progression as it left many of its victims blind, insane, and eventually dead.[4] Like the airmen's parachute, the deceptive operation hid in plain sight for decades until a whistleblower pulled the rip cord.

By the time the study was shut down in 1972, twenty-eight participants had died from syphilis, one hundred more had passed away from related complications, and at least forty spouses had been diagnosed with syphilis. The disease had also been transmitted to nineteen children at birth.[5]

Horrific as this experiment was, it was not the first time Black people were used as unwitting test subjects by the medical community—nor was it the last.

According to medical ethicist Harriet Washington, over the years, Black people have been

> . . . given experimental vaccines known to have
> unacceptably high lethality [rates] . . . enrolled
> in medical experiments without their consent or
> knowledge . . . subjected to surreptitious surgical
> and medical procedures while unconscious, injected
> with toxic substances, deliberately monitored rather
> than treated for deadly ailments, [and as with the
> Tuskegee participants] excluded from lifesaving
> treatments.[6]

Historically speaking, the medical field on the whole has been complicit in the inhumane treatment of Black people—from the assumption that Black people are inherently less intelligent than white people to the notion that the nerve endings of Blacks are less sensitive.[7] As recently as 2016, nearly half of first- and second-year medical students believed that Black people have thicker skin than white people and that Black people experience less pain. As a result, Black patients are 40 percent less likely to receive medication for acute pain than white patients.[8]

When it comes to childbirth, statistics show that Black women are three times more likely to die from pregnancy-related causes than white women. This disparity is caused in part by underlying chronic conditions such as hypertension and blood disorders, as well as a lack of access to prenatal testing and standardized health care.[9]

But in 2019, when Kirsten and I were living in New Orleans expecting our twins, *USA Today* published an exposé on the Touro Infirmary. This facility is located near one of the most impoverished areas of the city, which is also predominantly Black. Researchers found that Touro had one of the highest maternal mortality rates of any hospital in the country, pointing to inadequately trained doctors who failed to order proper tests, were slow to recognize emerging complications, and made surgical or medication mistakes. Officials at Touro, however, placed the blame on their patients' demographics, saying that lifestyle diseases, poor health, and poverty accounted for the high complication rates. In other words, the deaths were solely the mothers' fault.[10]

Given such a history (since these attitudes are not limited to New Orleans), it's no wonder many Black women harbor a distrust of medical professionals. It's also why for many Black women, being pro-choice does not represent some kind of genetic inclination toward killing their own offspring but rather reflects a deep-seated desire for bodily autonomy and control over their own future. The sad reality is that the road Black women have traveled since their arrival on American soil has been littered with medical assaults.

BREEDING MISTRUST

Anarcha, Betsey, and Lucy were three enslaved women who lived and worked on different plantations near Montgomery, Alabama, in the 1840s. After giving birth, each woman developed a painful medical condition that caused her to lose control of her bladder and bowels. Since there was no known cure, the women were told they would simply have to live with the pain for the rest of their lives.

This prognosis did not sit well with the men who owned them—not because they cared about the young women's welfare, but because their condition limited their productivity. So their owners sought the assistance of a local physician named Dr. J. Marion Sims.

Confident he could find a cure, Dr. Sims struck a deal with the men that would give him complete control over these women for the duration of their treatment.

One by one, the women were brought naked and restrained into an open operating room with dozens of medical students observing as they underwent a litany of experimental gynecological procedures. Because it was commonly believed that Black women did not experience pain to the same extent white women did, no anesthesia was administered—the women were fully awake for the duration.

Lucy's surgery resulted in an infection that not only failed to remedy her condition but caused ongoing pain. Betsey's and Anarcha's initial surgeries proved equally unsuccessful.

Over the next four years, Dr. Sims performed dozens of surgeries on the women—all experimental in nature. Finally, in 1849, on his thirtieth operation on Anarcha—using the tools and techniques he'd developed over the years of failed attempts—Dr. Sims cured her condition.

Dr. Sims's work earned him the moniker "the father of modern gynecology," though this accolade was gained through the pain, suffering, and exploitation of three powerless, defenseless women.[11]

Born on October 6, 1917, in Montgomery County, Mississippi, Fannie Lou Townsend was the youngest of twenty children. When she was six years old, she started working alongside her siblings picking cotton on a plantation in the Mississippi Delta. At the age of twenty-seven, she married fellow sharecropper Perry Hamer and looked forward to starting a family of her own.

After suffering devastating back-to-back stillbirths, Fannie Lou learned that she had a noncancerous uterine cyst. She scheduled to have it removed in hopes that the operation would allow her to have the children she and Perry so desperately desired.

When she awoke from the procedure, however, Fannie Lou was sickened to discover that instead of simply removing the tumor, her doctor had given her a complete hysterectomy. She would later learn that such practices of sterilizing young Black women without their consent were common.

Fannie Lou went on to become a prominent civil rights activist and eventually adopted four girls, one of whom later died of hemorrhaging after being refused admittance to a hospital due to her mother's activism.[12]

In March 1968, fourteen-year-old Elaine Riddick arrived at a hospital in Edenton, North Carolina, in labor with her first child after being raped by a man in her neighborhood. "He snatched me off the street and molested me, and threatened my life and said if I ever told anyone, that he would kill me," Riddick later shared.[13]

Frightened and alone, Riddick awoke hours later, wrapped in bandages. She was told that she had given birth to a baby boy. What she was not told was that immediately after her son was born, the doctor had cut and cauterized her fallopian tubes, rendering her sterile.

"They had approached my grandmother . . . and said that if she did not sign the X, they were going to stop her [welfare] supplements," Riddick explained. "My grandmother was illiterate. She had never, ever gone to school. She didn't understand what [the form] was, so she signed the X, and they did this to me."

It wasn't until she was undergoing a routine gynecological examination five years later that Riddick learned what had happened. "I asked the state of North Carolina why they did this to me, and they said it was because I was feebleminded, and that I would not be able to take care of myself. . . . They [said] that feeblemindedness is hereditary, so they sterilized me so I would not produce 'my kind.'"[14] Riddick later stated, "I am not feebleminded—I have never been feebleminded. . . . I was just a child who was raped. And then the state raped me all over again."[15]

The very notion that anyone has the right to take away a woman's ability to have children without their knowledge or consent is a complete violation of the most fundamental civil rights.

Yet what happened to women like Fannie Lou Hamer and Elaine Riddick was so commonplace in the South during the '60s and '70s that Hamer popularized the phrase "Mississippi appendectomy" to describe the involuntary sterilization of hundreds of thousands of unsuspecting young Black women under the guise of routine surgical procedures.

In fact, during the 1970s, unauthorized sterilization became the most rapidly growing form of birth control in the United States, rising from 200,000 cases in 1970 to more than 700,000 in 1980.[16] These sterilizations occurred under state-sanctioned eugenics laws designed to eliminate the reproduction of those considered "inferior" and "unfit," with some of America's largest philanthropic foundations and their namesakes fueling the movement.

Rather than addressing the crime, disease, and poverty that plague humanity, they instead opted to eliminate those they perceived to be the cause of the problem. As John D. Rockefeller stated, "The best philanthropy is constantly in search of the finalities—a search for cause, an attempt to cure evils at their source."[17]

Mississippi appendectomies and other forced sterilization techniques were machinations of the eugenics movement. Eugenics seeks to "breed out" disease, disabilities, and "so-called undesirable characteristics" from the population.[18] Although this movement is most frequently associated with Adolf Hitler, it was the American eugenics movement and

American racism that influenced the Nazi regime and their policies.[19] In Germany, this ethnic cleansing resulted in the targeted execution of more than six million Jews. While we may think we have moved well beyond such atrocities, the ideology behind eugenics has led to the slaughter of more than sixty-three million unborn children since the passing of *Roe v. Wade* in 1973.[20]

It is a well-known fact that the founder of Planned Parenthood, Margaret Sanger, had ties to the eugenics movement. In fact, many have argued that Sanger and her powerful, well-funded cohorts began Planned Parenthood as a means to eradicate what she termed the "defectives, delinquents and dependents" from society, primarily through sterilization and contraception.[21]

Though Planned Parenthood formally denounced Sanger in 2021, some, like Pro-Black Pro-Life founder Cherilyn Holloway, argue that Sanger's spirit lives on in Planned Parenthood's strident dedication to taking the lives of unborn children of color.

Planned Parenthood was planted with the seeds of eugenics, and that's the fruit we are seeing in our community. "The thing about systemic racism, in all of its facets, is that it is not something you can touch or see while it is happening because it is constantly working to oppress. Instead, what we see are the results of it. . . . That is why we see a disproportionate abortion rate in the black community; that is why we see them targeting our neighborhoods with subpar women's 'healthcare,' and that is why the systemic issues with Planned Parenthood run so deep."[22]

THE MEASURE OF A MAN

Rightly considered by many to be an act of genocide, the practice of selectively weeding out "undesirables" via involuntary sterilization is not only a crime against humanity but an outright denial of humanity. And although today most people would not openly endorse eugenics, we as a society are guilty of assigning value to people based on their perceived contribution to the world. We tend to think a person's worth rises and falls in accordance with their abilities, their prospective earning potential, and what we stand to gain or lose from them. Whether we admit it or not, we make these value calculations all the time, constantly asking ourselves, *How can this person help me?*

The NFL is very much a performance-based business, where a person's value depends on the answer to the question, "What have you done for me lately?" For a player, "lately" can mean your performance in the last game, the last practice, or even the last play. One week you're the hero, and the next you're the guy the media is raking over the coals and management wants to get rid of to free up a little cap space.

In 2004, I was drafted thirty-second overall by the New England Patriots. Needless to say, there were high expectations for me that year—not only from myself, but from the Patriots organization and the New England fan base. That summer, I went to Boston, worked hard in rookie minicamp, participated in OTAs, and had a solid training camp. The learning curve was steep and the competition intense, but I worked my tail off. By the time the preseason was over, I had earned significant playing time.

Our first regular season game that year was a Thursday Night matchup against the Indianapolis Colts at home, in Foxboro. We won the game 27–24, and I played well, catching two passes for sixteen yards. But after the game, my left knee was bothering me. I knew I had a slight MCL sprain going into the regular season, so just to be on the safe side, I got another MRI. It turned out I had torn my ACL. And just like that, my season was over. A week later, I had reconstructive surgery, and I spent the rest of the season on injured reserve.

By the way, there's a reason grown men break down in tears when they're loaded onto a cart and driven off the field with their head, neck, or leg immobilized. Yes, the injury itself hurts, but what hurts even more is knowing what lies ahead. Depending on the severity of the injury, you may not get to go to practice, attend regular team meetings, or work out with the rest of the team. And because the coaches, coordinators, and trainers have to put all their time and energy into the guys who are playing, you usually end up doing rehab on an entirely different schedule, sometimes outside the team facility. While each team is different, Coach Belichick didn't like to have unnecessary personnel hanging around on the sidelines, so even when I was finally able to walk around without crutches late in the season, I wasn't allowed to travel with the team or be on the field during home games. It was extremely isolating.

A few weeks into rehab, I ventured out to the mall on my crutches. I wasn't there long before a guy walked up to me and said, "Hey, man, sorry you got hurt. But, dude, you *totally* messed up my fantasy team."

Here I had just undergone major surgery—I was missing out on my entire rookie year, and I had no idea what my career was going to look like from this point forward—and this guy was worried about how my inability to play was impacting his fantasy football team. The moment I was no longer able to help him achieve his goals, I became expendable.

The Patriots went on to win the Super Bowl that year, but for me, the victory was bittersweet. While the occasion was definitely something to celebrate, I had missed all but one game, so I didn't feel as though I had contributed anything. In my mind, I barely felt like I was part of the team. For the longest time, I couldn't even bring myself to wear my Super Bowl ring. I just didn't feel like I'd earned it.

It wasn't until years later—after a lot of convincing from my teammates and my family, and after doing some spiritual wrestling on my own—that I realized even though my playing time had been limited that season, I was still a member of the 2004 New England Patriots team. My name was on that fifty-three-man roster. I had earned my spot. And regardless of whether I was a starter, a member of the practice squad, or an injured rookie with an ACL tear, I was still a Super Bowl champion simply by virtue of being a member of the team.

IMAGO DEI

Regardless of whether they can help you, every person who walks this earth has inherent value—not because of their earning potential, their IQ, or their athletic ability, but because they are created by God.

As human beings, we were created to reflect God's glory,

to serve as his ambassadors on earth, and to show the rest of the world what God is like. God made his intent clear from the very beginning:

> God said, "Let us make human beings in our image, to be like us. They will reign over the fish in the sea, the birds in the sky, the livestock, all the wild animals on the earth, and the small animals that scurry along the ground."
>
> So God created human beings in his own image.
>   In the image of God he created them;
>   male and female he created them.
> GENESIS 1:26-27

The fact that God gave us dominion over the rest of creation suggests that we are connected to him in ways that animals are not. We have a purpose; we have a destiny.

> You saw me before I was born.
>   Every day of my life was recorded in your book.
> Every moment was laid out
>   before a single day had passed.
> PSALM 139:16

We—all of us—are his image bearers, regardless of age, gender, race, ethnicity, education, financial status, ability, disability, church affiliation, or political party. And because we are made in the image of our Creator, our lives are inherently valuable and imbued with dignity.

In a sermon entitled "The American Dream," Martin Luther King Jr. said,

> The whole concept of the *imago dei*, as it is expressed in Latin, the "image of God," is the idea that all men have something within them that God injected. Not that they have substantial unity with God, but that every man has a capacity to have fellowship with God. And this gives him a uniqueness, it gives him worth, it gives him dignity. And we must never forget this as a nation: There are no gradations in the image of God. Every man from a treble white to a bass black is significant on God's keyboard, precisely because every man is made in the image of God. One day we will learn that. We will know one day that God made us to live together as brothers and to respect the dignity and worth of every man.[23]

That's why we lament the injustices of Jim Crow laws and why we find slavery and racism reprehensible. It's why we are outraged by mass genocides such as the Holocaust and those in Rwanda, Cambodia, and Darfur. It's why we grieve when there are murders in our cities and on our streets. It's why we weep when we learn about yet another school shooting or hate crime, or about an adolescent who has taken their own life because of bullying. It's why we mourn the sixty-three million preborn children who have been killed since the passing of *Roe v. Wade*.

It's because of the image of God.

Though sin has marred the perfect image we once bore, we are still image bearers of God, imbued with eternal significance and undeniable worth.

Some would claim that a child who grows up poor, unwanted, or uneducated is better off not growing up at all. In fact, doctors routinely encourage parents to terminate pregnancies when prenatal screening and diagnostic testing reveal the possibility of an anomaly such as Down syndrome or another congenital condition. Underpinning this recommendation is the idea that a child's worth is determined by their statistical probability to achieve our society's predetermined metrics of success. Their worth and value are based solely on their projected contributions to society.

But everyone—man, woman, and child—has inherent value that transcends age, ethnicity, ability, and development. This worth is not something that can be earned, transferred, or lost. It is an irremovable, irrevocable stamp, embossed on each of us by a Creator who saw fit to make men and women in his own image.

IS ANYBODY LISTENING?

For ten years, I served on the executive committee of the NFL Players Association (NFLPA). Comprised of former players, active players, and a host of legal and business professionals, the NFLPA represents and protects players' rights with regard to salaries, health and safety measures, and overall working conditions. That covers everything from meal prep, locker room cleanliness, and equipment maintenance to limiting the number of full-pad practices teams are allowed to have and making sure the terms of the collective bargaining agreement are met. They also advocate for compensation for players who suffer career-ending injuries, ensuring that former players are provided with the physical, emotional, and professional support they need to succeed in life after football.

Prior to the formation of the NFLPA, the league and individual team owners wielded all the power. Make no mistake: while football is a sport, the NFL is a business, generating upward of $17 billion a year in TV deals, ticket sales, and merchandise.[24] And in a sport where every snap carries with it the potential for a career-ending injury, somebody needed to be thinking about what was in the best interest of the players, advocating on their behalf.

What makes the NFLPA work is that it is made up of the very people it is designed to protect. As players, we understand from experience the violent nature of the game and the impact it can have on our health. That's what makes us such powerful advocates for one another. Much of the progress that has been made in terms of concussion protocol, helmet technology, and chronic traumatic encephalopathy (CTE) prevention, for example, has been championed by the NFLPA.

In 2009, when we were playing the Broncos, I took a big hit that resulted in a concussion. The training staff asked if I was okay, and I mumbled something to the effect of "Yeah . . . I don't know." They told me to take a seat on the bench.

I spent the remainder of the game sitting under the hot afternoon sun in a noisy stadium—at altitude—feeling embarrassed, like I should just suck it up and go back into the game. But at the same time, I worried about the damage that had already been done.

Flash forward to 2019—I was now with the Saints and we were playing the Rams in the NFC Championship game. One of our tight ends took a hit and stumbled a bit getting up. He was immediately pulled from the game, his helmet was taken away, and the team physician and NFLPA-approved, unaffiliated (that is, not paid by either team) neurotrauma consultant performed a sideline survey. The player's speech and eye movements were checked, and he was asked a series of Maddocks questions ("What city are we in?" "What quarter is it?" "What's the score?" "Who did we play last week?") to check his short-term memory. Then he was taken to the locker room for a more thorough neurological exam.

Typically, if players pass the sideline exam, they'll be able to go back into the game and the staff will just keep a close eye on them. But even though he passed all his sideline tests, as well as a complete locker-room neurological exam, the trainers didn't let him back into the game. He was exhibiting gross motor instability—in other words, his gait was off. So as much as he wanted to go back onto the field, and as much as we could have used him out there, his day was over—championship game or not.

By the way, that's why they take your helmet away when you get hurt: to keep you from going back in of your own accord. Because believe me, guys will try. There's a fine line between being a gladiator and being a human being, and the NFLPA's job is to uplift the humanity of players and advocate for their well-being, no matter the cost.

Contrast this level of care with what was provided to Missouri congresswoman Cori Bush as a teen. When she was nineteen years old, she found herself faced with an unplanned pregnancy. Having just started college, she decided to get an abortion—her second, in fact. The first one came after she was sexually assaulted at seventeen.

"I thought I was ready," Bush said in an interview. "[I] was thinking . . . *Okay, you've done this before, you know the rooms, you know what it looks like, you know what it feels like in this place, you know what to expect.* . . . I got to [that] room; I was helped up onto the table by the nurse . . . I just felt like I needed more time, so I said, 'No, you know what, I'm not ready.' And the nurse just wouldn't listen to me, and I said, 'No, I'm not ready,' and as I'm saying no, they continue to pull the instruments and get everything ready." The next thing she knew, the procedure had started. Bush frantically scanned the room hoping to catch the eye of someone who would help her or speak out on her behalf, but "they absolutely ignored me—even to the point of [telling me to] calm down, as if *I* was the problem."

As a young Black woman, Bush said she felt voiceless, and as if she were being told, "You don't know what you need. We know better."[25]

Years later, when Bush was five months pregnant, she went to see her doctor for a routine prenatal visit after suffering four months of severe, almost constant pain and morning sickness. As she was sitting in the waiting room, she noticed a sign on the wall that said, "If you feel like something is wrong, something is wrong. Tell your doctor." So that's what she did.

Bush says, "I told her that I was having severe pains, and she said, 'Oh no, you're fine. You're fine, go home, and I'll see you next time.'"

A week later, Bush went into premature labor and gave birth to a one-pound, three-ounce baby boy.

"His ears were still in his head, his eyes were still fused shut, his fingers were smaller than rice, and his skin was translucent. A Black baby with translucent skin. You could see his lungs. He could fit within the palm of my hand."

Though her son was given a zero percent chance of survival, he was resuscitated, and after four months in neonatal care, he was able to come home.

A short time later, sixteen weeks pregnant with her second child, Bush went in for an ultrasound and was told that once again she was experiencing premature labor.

Frantic, Bush pleaded with the doctor to do something— anything—to save her child. Instead, he told her, "Just go home. Let it abort. You can get pregnant again because that's what you people do." And with that, the doctor left.

Bush was beside herself. When her sister, who had come to the appointment with her, learned what had happened, she was so incensed she picked up a nearby chair and literally hurled it down the hallway.

"Nurses came running from everywhere to see what was wrong," says the congresswoman. "A nurse called my doctor, and she put me on a stretcher."

The next morning, Bush's doctor performed a surgical stitch to close Bush's uterus so she could carry the baby to term. Both of Bush's children are now healthy, thriving adults, but she is aware how close she came to losing both of them because her medical providers were unwilling to listen to her.

"This is what desperation looks like," says Bush. "[A] chair flying down the hallway. This is what being your own advocate looks like. Every day black women are subjected to harsh and racist treatment during pregnancy and childbirth. Every day black women die because the system denies our humanity."[26]

NO VOICE, NO CHOICE

Given the long, sordid history of neglect and abuse Black people have suffered in a medical context, it's small wonder so many harbor a mistrust of the medical community.

This is, in part, why many pro-choice advocates, including Bush, say, "My body, my choice." It's not that Black women don't value life or that they don't love or want children. The problem is that, historically, *their* lives have not been valued.

A young Black woman who walks into a doctor's office can't be certain whether she'll be listened to, whether her complaints will be taken seriously, and whether she'll receive the proper treatment. This skepticism has been ingrained over hundreds of years.

So for many women, being pro-choice is not about shirking responsibility or having a brazen disregard for human life. It's about gaining autonomy and control in an area where, historically, both have been stripped away. It's not simply a matter of saying, "I want the right to be able to end my child's life." It's about yelling from the rooftops, "No matter what I decide, *I* want to decide. I want to control this!"

But the issue goes even deeper. Black women are also living in a society that does not, on the whole, value their lives. Many are living in poverty, with limited support systems. They're alone. They're frightened. They can't see a way out of their situation. And the thought of bringing a child into that world feels untenable at best. Once again, it's not that they don't value life—they do. That's precisely why for many young Black women, abortion feels like their *only* choice.

Cherilyn Holloway says that if we want women to see the life inside them as having a life, then "we have to create an environment in which [that baby] can thrive. Because right now, [the mother] is in an environment where she feels oppressed, and that's why she's fighting for *her* life."[27]

In order to do that, we need to develop a little empathy.

CHAPTER 4

HAVE A LITTLE EMPATHY

You never really understand a person until you consider things from his point of view . . . until you climb into his skin and walk around in it.

HARPER LEE

We lived in New Orleans for four years while I was playing football for the Saints. Our daughter Eden and our twins, Asher and Levi, were born there, so that city and the relationships we forged will always have a special place in our hearts. It was also where our children first encountered the reality of homelessness and poverty that so many men, women, and children deal with on a daily basis.

Not long after we moved there and started to establish a regular cadence of work, school, and weekend activities, Kirsten and I were both struck by the large population of homeless people. We saw them under overpasses when we went downtown and meandering through streets and parking lots as we made our way to the Superdome on game days.

I distinctly remember a family we frequently saw on Carrollton Avenue, where Grace took ballet lessons, and another couple near the I-10 exit in Metairie, where we rented a home near the Saints training facility. At some point Kirsten decided that, as a family, we should get involved.

One night I came home from practice to find our living room floor covered in toiletries, snacks, Bibles, and small envelopes filled with petty cash. Our kids had a little assembly line, packing gallon-sized Ziploc bags with small gifts to meet both physical and spiritual needs.

Kirsten called them "blessing bags," and after packing about twenty, we loaded them into the car. The next morning, while I was at practice, Kirsten drove the kids to the places we'd noticed homeless people congregating and passed them out.

When Kirsten rolled down her window to pass out the first blessing bag at the I-10 underpass, the kids were, understandably, on edge. After all, they didn't know the recipients, and most didn't look like the people they typically associated with.

Truth be told, that's part of the reason we included the kids in this activity. Micah 6:8 tells us to "love mercy," and part of loving mercy is being drawn to people who are in distress and loving people who others might shy away from. We wanted our kids to learn how to serve people they didn't know, without expecting anything in return.

Kirsten and the kids did this once a month, and between outings, they kept a few blessing bags in the car as they ran errands. After handing out bags a few times and seeing the gratitude on the faces of the people they were helping, the kids became the loudest backseat philanthropists in the city, competing with one another to find people they thought could use a small gift of love.

From time to time, after Kirsten rolled the window up and the recipient was out of earshot, the kids would ask her, "Why doesn't that person have a home?"

She would respond, "I don't know, baby. Everyone has a story, and I don't know theirs." She's right—we don't know the circumstances in someone's life that led them to a place of desperation. I've heard stories of people who are just barely getting by and then they have a medical emergency or get laid off from work. Their entire savings is depleted and they can't afford rent, and just like that, they're out on the street. Other people are well-off, but when the stock market shifts, they wake up with nothing. Others prefer living on the streets over being in an abusive home. Then there are those battling addiction who struggle to break the cycle. There are countless reasons people find themselves in dire situations, and unless we take the time to get acquainted with them, we'll never know. Sadly, our human nature is to assume the worst.

AN ADVANTAGEOUS LESSON

I fully acknowledge that because of my career, my kids enjoy certain privileges that others don't, financial and otherwise. After home games, for example, my kids used to come onto the field to run around with the other players' kids. It was the coolest thing to see guys like Drew Brees chasing them around and throwing passes to them. The only reason they were allowed to be there was because their father played in the National Football League. The kids who belonged to the sixty thousand other people at the game didn't have the same opportunity.

Being able to run on the field at the Superdome or at Gillette Stadium is a privilege our kids had because we as players opened the door for them and granted them access, in much the same way that some people have had certain doors opened for them because of their ancestors, their socio-economic status, or the color of their skin.

There's a myth of superiority as much as there's a myth of inferiority in our society, and both are problematic. That's why I began this book with a brief overview of the Reconstruction era and highlighted some of the ways Black people, in particular, have been victimized by a largely white power structure. It's also why I took my kids to the lynching memorial and why I teach them about things like Black Wall Street and the Red Summers of Terror. And it's why Kirsten and I make sure they know about people like Frederick Douglass, Mary Jackson, Katherine Johnson, Charles Drew, and Mae Jemison.

So much of history is relegated to the shadows. If we aren't familiar with the atrocities of the past, we can't fully understand how we got to where we are today and why some people struggle more than others do. And if we don't teach our kids about all the great things Black people have done despite their circumstances, they may never fully realize what they're capable of achieving.

When kids who live in the inner city look around and see nothing but terrible schools, crime, poverty, and unemployment, they begin to think that they are pathologically relegated to that lifestyle—and that's all they're capable of.

Likewise, when you grow up white, middle class, and third- or fourth-generation college educated, you're not always aware of the policies and programs that have benefited your family over the years. This can lead to a false sense of superiority that blinds you to the difficulties other people face, making you reluctant to lend a helping hand.

None of us got to decide when, where, or to whom we were born. Nor were we given the choice of what color our skin would be.

Kirsten and I want our kids to be tenderhearted. We want them to be responsible with whatever blessings or privileges God has given them and to assist those who may not have had those same privileges. Because no matter which side of the poverty line we're on, the ground before the cross is level. We all need the blood of Christ. We are equal under God, and we all have the same inherent value, no matter our skin color or situation. This spiritual truth not only mandates our fight for fairness for the disenfranchised but empowers us to do so with divine wisdom, persistent courage, and extraordinary empathy.

When I see a father on the side of the road asking for money so he can take care of his kids, I may not be able to identify with his specific situation, but I can identify with his humanity. He wants to be a good parent for his kids, just like I do. I acknowledge his humanity in the same way I would want mine to be acknowledged. It's not a matter of thinking,

I'm better than you. It's simply acknowledging the reality that *I'm better off than you today.* Because the fact of the matter is, any of us could fall on hard times at any moment. Frankly, I would hope someone would be gracious enough to help me if I needed it.

THE GOOD SAMARITAN

No matter the circumstances, we should all have an emotional response when we see human suffering. The plight of others should invoke our sympathy, compassion, and concern. But too often, our minds fill in the blanks in a way that caters to our biases instead of allowing our hearts to address the pain point first. Callousness is not becoming of people who call themselves believers. In fact, it is blatant disobedience—and evidence of a heart grown cold.

In an often-referenced biblical account, Jesus encountered an expert in Mosaic law who decided to test him about eternal life. "Teacher," he said, "what must I do to inherit eternal life?"

Jesus answered, "What is written in the law?"

The lawyer replied, "Love the Lord your God with all your heart, with all your soul, with all your strength, and with all your mind, and your neighbor as yourself."

Jesus affirmed this answer, but the man, wanting to justify himself, asked Jesus, "Who is my neighbor?"

Instead of directly answering the question, Jesus replied not only to the man but to the entire crowd of onlookers, who were likely waiting for his rebuke.

Jesus then told the story of a man who was stripped,

beaten, and left half dead by robbers as he traveled from Jerusalem to Jericho. As the man lay on death's doorstep, a priest who happened to be traveling the same way saw him. But instead of helping the man, he crossed to the other side of the road and passed by. Similarly, a Levite (another religious official) arrived on the scene. Upon seeing the injured man, he also decided to pass by on the other side.

It's probably worth noting that, unlike the more "flock-centered" pastors and priests we have today, the priests of Jesus' day were primarily responsible for interpreting the law and officiating in the Temple. Regardless, one would think that stopping to help an injured man on the side of the road would be an act of sheer human decency.

Still, if the crowd was stunned by the callous response of the two holy men, I'm sure they were even less prepared for what Jesus said next.

"But a Samaritan on his journey came up to him," he continued. "When he saw the man, he had compassion." This revelation surely drew an audible gasp from the crowd, as the Jews despised the Samaritans. They were considered half-breeds, the descendants of intermarriages between foreigners and the Israelites left behind during the Assyrian exile.

The Samaritan soothed the injured man's wounds with olive oil and wine before bandaging him up. Then he put the man on his own donkey and brought him to an inn. The Samaritan gave the innkeeper money and told him, "Take care of this man. If his bill runs higher than this, I'll pay you the next time I'm here."

I can only imagine what the lawyer must have been thinking by the time Jesus concluded the parable. I'm sure he was frantically contemplating the story's meaning and thinking through his response when Jesus asked him, "Which of these three do you think proved to be a neighbor to the man who fell into the hands of the robbers?"

"The one who showed mercy to him," he answered.

Jesus told him, "Go and do the same" (see Luke 10:25-37).

Jesus calls us to demonstrate compassion not simply because it's the right thing to do but because it's an inseparable part of a godly life. The greatest commandments are to "love the Lord your God with all your heart, all your soul, and all your mind and to love your neighbor as yourself" (see Matthew 22:37-39). The rewards of heaven and the fullness of life here on earth are made manifest when we reflect our vertical relationship and love for God through our horizontal relationships and love for people.

When we devote our time, talent, and treasure to loving God, the overflow will be a compassionate, righteous sense of responsibility and a passion for seeking the well-being of those around us, whether they are of our ilk or not.

I believe that's why Jesus talked about a Samaritan—an outcast—to drive his point home. The Jewish victim's neighbor was not someone in the religious elite, whose immersion in Mosaic law should have helped him understand the importance of service and kindness. It was not the members who shared a similar heritage and ethnic background, which should have conjured at least an ounce of concern when they saw one of their own bleeding and alone. Rather, the good neighbor was the one no one would have expected.

In telling this story, Jesus was teaching his followers to exhibit the kind of countercultural, counter-religious love and advocacy that transcends the world's boundaries and expectations. We are not only to express sympathy for the hardships of others but also to empathize with them by putting ourselves in their shoes. The Samaritan matched the movement of his feet with the movement of his emotions, sparing no expense or effort to right a wrong he had no part in making.

Jesus didn't provide exhaustive details in this parable. As I read this passage, I can't help but speculate about the unspoken thoughts of the priest and the Levite as they passed by. Perhaps they didn't want to become ceremonially unclean en route to Jerusalem by going too close to what might have been a dead body. This would have been understandable, considering the requirements of Levitical law. Or maybe they knew that the man's condition would require a time commitment they weren't willing to make due to other pressing matters. Or perhaps they considered it safer to move as quickly as possible down this dangerous road, lest they encounter the same fate as this poor fellow. I hope my worst assumption isn't true—that they simply didn't care about a person outside their circle who couldn't benefit them in any way.

Though the parable is typically called "the Good Samaritan," Jesus was speaking directly to the religious leaders, exposing their hypocrisy and challenging them to change. Juxtaposed against the two who walked past, the Samaritan was a man of intervening action. He tangibly exhibited the justice, mercy, and faithfulness the others professed but neglected when it came to their actions. We have no record of the Samaritan interrogating the victim about where he'd been hanging out, his bad habits, or his morals.

He wasted no time preaching piety or casting blame. Instead, the Samaritan changed his schedule, broke away from his cultural norms, opened his heart, and shared his resources to help a stranger in a time of desperate need.

Those of us who desire to be good neighbors should "go and do the same."

MISCONCEPTIONS

In 2019, I had the opportunity to visit the Louisiana State Penitentiary. I went with a small group, led by a friend I met during my time with the Baltimore Ravens who currently serves as chaplain for the Buffalo Bills. Often referred to as Angola Prison, as it was built on an old plantation site worked mostly by enslaved people from the African country of Angola, this penitentiary has the dubious distinction of being one of the most violent and horrific prisons in the United States.

At one point, our group visited death row. In recent years, there has been less of an emphasis on solitary confinement, but in the past, inmates on death row would spend twenty-three hours a day in eight-by-ten windowless concrete cells. They were allowed to leave for only one hour a day to shower, make phone calls, walk the corridor of their cellblock, or sit outside in a small, locked cage—all of which they did alone. They had no contact with anyone other than the prison staff. And some of these guys were there for decades.[1]

As we walked the dingy cellblocks (with no air-conditioning), surrounded by nothing but concrete and steel, the full brunt of the Louisiana heat and humidity bore down on us. Today, Angola spans eighteen thousand acres, most of it farm fields of wheat, corn, soybeans, and cotton, picked and harvested by the incarcerated for a few cents an hour as horse-mounted guards oversee their progress.[2]

As I witnessed the scene before me, I couldn't help but be reminded of the exception for slavery, which was cleverly crafted into the thirteenth amendment: "except as a punishment for crime." I looked at the faces of the inmates we engaged with during our brief visit, 73 percent of whom were Black.[3]

I pictured the hundreds of enslaved men and women who had been ripped from their homes and forced—under an unparalleled system of cruelty—to work the very land I was standing on. I flashed forward to the era of convict leasing and finally to the mass incarceration that continues to confine their descendants in institutions like this one. As the history of this place washed over me, I felt the full gravity of what it represented.

Louisiana has one of the highest exoneration rates in the country, fueled by a legacy of wrongful conviction.[4] Even so, most of the men we encountered readily admitted their transgressions and knew they deserved consequences. Most of them were there for a reason, and based on their actions, they deserved to be removed from society for a time before being reintegrated into the community. But they were still human beings. They were still made in God's image. And they retained their dignity as human beings. I couldn't help but think that animals in the zoo received more humane treatment than men in this prison historically had.

We have a tendency to put people into categories that are almost nonhuman—especially when we can't understand why they act in a way that seems objectionable to us.

Likewise, there are a lot of misconceptions when it comes to abortion-determined women. Some people assume that these women don't care about children, that they don't experience guilt or remorse over their decision to terminate a pregnancy, or that they are selfish degenerates who use abortion flippantly, as a form of birth control.

I hear these arguments a lot. I have also met many of these women, and these arguments don't ring true. On the contrary, the vast majority of abortion-minded women I've met say they would prefer to parent but feel as though their life circumstances give them no other choice.

They worry that their other children, who are already doing without so much, would suffer even more. Many lack emotional support from their families, financial support from the fathers, spiritual support from their church, and social support from their community. Many describe abortion as the most difficult, heartrending decision they've ever had to make. And those who have had abortions suffer years, sometimes decades, of debilitating guilt, depression, and remorse. These women are not the cold, calculating villains they've been made out to be. They are frightened. They are desperate. And many are all alone.

While many of the abortion statistics point to women of color who fall into lower income brackets, they are not the only ones.

Years ago, I spoke at a pregnancy center in an affluent area of Georgia. One of the women who worked there told me,

"Well-to-do women will pull up in their Mercedes—many of whom are married with several children—to get abortions."

Prior to the passage of *Roe* in 1973, middle- and upper-middle-class women were the only ones who could afford to get legal abortions. It wasn't until then that the procedure became more accessible to women with less means. According to recent data, 75 percent of abortion patients live at or below the poverty line. Studies show that as income levels increase, abortion rates decrease, with women in the highest income groups representing less than half the national abortion rate.[5]

According to the Dallas-based nonprofit Human Coalition, which rescues preborn children and their families from abortion, the average abortion-determined client they serve is twenty-nine years old, is single, already has at least one child, does not have a college degree, is unemployed or works part-time, and is from an ethnic minority.

Contrary to what many might believe, Christians aren't immune. Studies have shown that four in ten women who have abortions are regular churchgoers.[6] So it's not just happening outside the church. Abortion-determined and post-abortive women are sitting right next to us in the pews more often than we think.

Some people look at these factors—generational poverty, lack of health care and insurance, mistrust of the medical community—and say, "Because of these reasons, abortion should be a woman's right. It's her body and her choice, and no one should be able to tell her differently. She's likely dealing with the impact of dozens of variables, each compounding the other." Others see the same information and say,

"I don't care what the mother is dealing with—her preborn child is still a human being and deserves to live." In a sense, they're both right, and they're both wrong.

Don't get me wrong—I am 100 percent pro-life. But I also understand the myriad factors that impact a woman's decision.

Not everybody has a strong nuclear family or support system. Not everyone has a savings account or stock options as a safety net. Not everyone is able to go to college. Most minimum-wage jobs don't offer health plans, profit sharing, paid time off, or 401(k)s. Not everyone has access to transportation and childcare. Some people are supporting not just themselves but extended family.

The point is, we don't always have a complete understanding of what someone else is going through. And whether a woman decides to abort her child or not, she still has value before God. She's not to be demonized. The way we speak about people who do things that we consider to be wrong says a lot about us.

In the book *Compassion (&) Conviction*, Justin Giboney writes, "As Christians, we have to be careful about how we label people. When we portray others in a demeaning light, we sin against them and reveal our own lack of wisdom (Proverbs 11:12). Discrediting a group might help us win an argument, but if it belittles our neighbor, it's wrong."[7]

Simply put, we are called to "rejoice with those who rejoice" and "weep with those who weep" (Romans 12:15, ESV); to "bear one another's burdens" (Galatians 6:2, ESV); and to "be kind to one another, tenderhearted, forgiving one another, as God in Christ forgave [us]" (Ephesians 4:32 ESV).

INCONCEIVABLE

When we were filming the documentary I mentioned in chapter 1, I flew to Washington, DC, for a few days to tape some interviews. I decided to bring along my two oldest daughters, Naomi and Grace, who were nine and ten.

Because Kirsten and I were both executive producers, we'd been discussing the documentary a lot around the house, and I wanted the girls to understand what we were doing and why. So one night after dinner, I sat them down for a talk.

"Mommy and I are doing a documentary about the issue of abortion," I said. "That means Daddy has to go interview some people in Washington, DC. I'd like you to come with me."

They looked at each other and then back at me. "What's abortion?" Naomi asked.

"Abortion is when a doctor kills the baby while it's still inside the mother so it can't be born."

That really threw them.

"Why would anyone do that?" they asked, horrified.

"Well, some people do it because they feel like they aren't ready to be parents yet," I explained. "Or they don't have enough money to take care of a baby. Or sometimes they just don't want a baby."

Grace tilted her head in confusion. "But why would somebody not want their child?" To her, the very notion that someone wouldn't want a baby was inconceivable.

Babies have always been a cause for celebration in the Watson house.

In December of 2008, when Kirsten was eight months pregnant with Grace, I was three thousand miles away, playing the Seahawks in Seattle. It was the first of two games we would be playing on the West Coast over a ten-day stretch, so Coach Belichick decided that instead of flying the whole team back to Boston after the game, we would stay out West for the following week's game against the Raiders.

While I didn't mind forgoing back-to-back cross-country trips, as a first-time dad, I *was* nervous about leaving Kirsten at home by herself.

Midway through the second quarter of the game against the Seahawks, Matt Cassel threw me a short pass down the middle for a touchdown. I figured as long as I was in the end zone, I would give Kirsten a shout-out to let her know I was thinking about her. So I found the closest TV camera, stuffed the ball under the front of my jersey to mimic a baby bump, and rubbed my belly.

It was a great moment—until the flags came out and I got called for unsportsmanlike conduct, forcing us to back up ten yards on the ensuing kickoff. Needless to say, Coach Belichick was not happy. Neither was the League. They fined me ten grand for that little end zone celebration. They eventually reduced it to five thousand dollars after I explained why I'd done it, but either way, it was worth every penny.

I was thrilled about becoming a father. I even framed the fine letter I received from the League and hung it up in Grace's nursery next to a picture someone took of me in the end zone.

That was the one year out of the six I played with the Patriots at the beginning of my career that we didn't make the playoffs. Even though Tom Brady had torn his ACL in the season opener, we still went 11–5 under Matt. Normally that would have been more than enough to get in, but apparently God knew I needed to be home that season.

Grace's due date was February 2, which happened to be Super Bowl Sunday that year. She was born two days early, on January 31. We watched the big game as a family of three, cuddled together on the tiny recovery-room bed at Brigham and Women's hospital. Had we gone all the way, I might have missed out on one of the greatest days of my life.

One of the good things about football is that if you hang around long enough, things tend to evolve. By 2018, I was back in New Orleans playing with the Saints and the NFL had relaxed its end zone celebration rules. It couldn't have happened at a better time.

The past two years had been tough for Kirsten and me. I tore my Achilles tendon on the first play of the Ravens' third preseason game against the Lions and missed the entire 2016 season. The following year, Kirsten suffered two miscarriages. We were devastated.

But now we were back in New Orleans, and both the Watsons and the Saints were having a great season. We were on a six-game winning streak, and Kirsten and I had just learned that we were expecting twins. Kirsten was only about thirteen weeks along, so aside from our siblings, we hadn't told anybody yet.

Our next game was a Sunday-nighter at home, against the Los Angeles Rams, and unlike the Seattle game, this time Kirsten was sitting in the front row. With a little over a minute to play in the first half, Drew Brees threw me a perfect pass over the right side of the defense, and I ran it into the end zone for a touchdown.

Now, tight ends don't get into the end zone anywhere near as often as wide receivers or running backs, so I didn't know when or if I would have this opportunity again. I thought, *I might as well take advantage of this.* So once again, I stuffed the ball under my jersey, gave it a little rub, looked right at Kirsten, and held up five fingers to represent the kids we already had, then two more for the twins.

I didn't get fined this time, but poor Kirsten spent the rest of the game responding to frantic texts and phone calls from pretty much everybody we knew. After the game (which we won, by the way), Kirsten just shook her head and said, "You know, you could have at least told me you were going to do that."

I just laughed and said, "Babe, even I didn't know I was going to do that."

A few weeks later, Kirsten went to the doctor to find out if we were having boys, girls, or one of each. Normally I would have gone with her, but we had practice that day, so I told her to FaceTime me once she was there. I'd watch right along with her if I could.

I'd just finished getting dressed and was about to head onto the field when she called.

"Is now a good time?" she asked.

Honestly, it wasn't. The locker room was packed, guys were getting dressed and joking around, music was blasting—it was pretty much organized chaos.

So, of course, I said, "Now's perfect."

She turned the camera so I could see the ultrasound screen, and the technician started moving the wand around. After five kids, I thought I was well versed in ultrasound technology. I could usually decipher all the important body parts, and I sometimes joked that I didn't need to pay the professionals anymore.

But this time, with two babies, it was different. Their busy black-and-white images blended together, making it difficult to tell what was happening.

The technician stopped the wand and said, "Okay, do you want to know the sex?"

We both said, "Definitely."

The technician pointed to something on the screen, and Kirsten gasped. "Oh my gosh, babe, can you see it?"

Honestly, I couldn't see a thing. But the fact that she asked if I could see "it" gave me a clue.

"It's a boy?" I asked.

"Boys," the technician corrected, rotating the wand again. "You're having identical twin boys."

Man, I lost it. I turned around, held up the phone, and yelled, "Hey, y'all, hey! I'm having two boys! I'm having two boys!"

The whole locker room erupted in applause, and everyone started screaming. "Yeah!" "That's awesome!" "Congratulations!" It was incredible. I wish I had it on film.

The point is, we've never been more devastated than when we experienced our two miscarriages, and we were never happier or more excited than when we learned we were expecting each of our seven kids. So I could understand why the girls were at such a loss as to why anyone would be less than ecstatic about the prospect of welcoming a new baby into the world.

"I know it's hard for you to imagine," I reassured them as we were preparing for our trip to DC. "It's hard for me too. That's why I'd like you to come along and meet some of the people who are dealing with this. Like Mommy always says, 'Everybody has a story.'"

At the filming, the crew was extremely accommodating. My daughters learned how all the equipment worked, and they even got a film credit for their help holding one of the light reflector umbrellas.

We interviewed dozens of women over the course of the filming, but one in particular made an impact on my girls. It happened on the second day of filming.

The interviews were conducted at a local hotel, and because of the way the lights were set up, Naomi and Grace had to sit behind a partition. This meant they couldn't see the woman being interviewed. But as soon as she started speaking, they were absolutely riveted. We all were.

This woman shared that she'd had five abortions by the age of twenty. Complications resulting from the fifth one had almost cost her her life. Now she's a fierce advocate for other post-abortive women. As she spoke, she fought back tears over the emotional toll her abortions have taken on her and the judgment she has faced when sharing her story.

It was an incredibly moving interview. At several points, even the film crew broke down. When we took a break so everyone could collect themselves, my girls waved me over from behind the partition. With their eyes wide, they asked, "Daddy, can we please meet her?"

Mind you, when I interviewed prominent activists, my daughters were polite but quietly sat off set coloring or reading. They were equally unimpressed with the senators and congress members I spoke to. But her story really got to them. They connected with the emotion they heard in her voice, and they were moved by her love and care for other women. They were struck by the strength of a woman who was willing to take hit after hit for her past if it meant helping others.

I introduced the girls to her, and she spoke with them for a few minutes. They even took a picture together, which we texted to Kirsten.

My daughters might not have fully understood why this young woman made the decisions she made, but they were able to see her pain and struggles. She wasn't a monster. She was a breathing, feeling, hurting human being who was every bit as devastated by the loss of her children as Kirsten and I had been.

I recently brought Naomi with me to a Human Coalition event, and—of her own volition—she decided to donate some of her own money to support women contemplating abortion.

Familiarity with the plight of others influences how we react to them. When we encounter a homeless person living under an overpass or a frightened young woman faced with an unexpected pregnancy, our reaction will likely be measured when it's not us, or someone like us. The goal is to develop the kind of empathy that extends beyond our personal experience and allows us to embrace others' circumstances as if they were our own.

God hears every groan and sees every tear. As human beings created in his likeness, so must we. Because only when we truly empathize with the plight of others are we moved to help.

GO AND DO THE SAME

In moments of crisis and life-altering decisions, abortion-determined women don't need judgment or condemnation.

They need compassionate action that will address the complex web of circumstances that make them vulnerable to irreversible, heart-shattering decisions.

This is not to absolve individuals of personal responsibility. Rather, it's about shifting our own perspective—humbly putting ourselves in another person's situation. We adopt a posture of love toward others because Christ loved us. We listen to women who would prefer to parent if their circumstances were different, and we empower them to choose life. And like the Good Samaritan, we open our hearts and share our resources to save lives and make right what we had no role in making wrong.

We have to be willing to be uncomfortable. This means saying, "I'm willing to invest time in getting to know this woman. I'm willing to find out what she's dealing with and what she needs help with." It's saying, "I'm willing to listen without judging and show compassion for her plight. I'm willing to make a long-term commitment that may not be convenient or easy for me. I'm even willing to be let down from time to time. And even if I'm disappointed, I won't give up. I'll do what's right, no matter how hard it is, for as long as it takes."

That's where it gets dicey for some people, and that's why this is hard work.

Making abortion unthinkable and unnecessary will cost us something. To promote human flourishing in a world bent on human demise will take fortitude, sacrifice, and strategic planning. But if children and mothers are worth it—and I believe they are—crossing to the other side of the road is not an option.

CHAPTER 5

THE POWER OF ONE

I am no longer accepting the things I cannot change.
I am changing the things I cannot accept.

ANGELA Y. DAVIS

The great Vince Lombardi once described football as a game
of inches. Sure, sometimes there's a huge breakaway play
where a guy finds a hole, slips a tackle, and runs fifty or sixty
yards for a touchdown. But more often than not, every yard
gained is a battle. One link in the chain can mean the difference between continuing a game-winning drive or turning
over the ball on downs. No matter the score, no matter how
much time is left on the clock, and no matter how much
the odds are stacked against you, you have to keep moving
forward. That's the only way to win.

Despite the fact that *Roe* has been overturned, roughly 75
percent of the country is still very abortion friendly. And in
the dozen or so states where abortion has been completely

banned, many companies and employers are helping women get to a state where abortion is still legal, some even paying for their travel and offsetting additional expenses not covered by their health plans.[1]

Meanwhile, Planned Parenthood, the country's single largest abortion provider, is increasing its efforts, launching new mobile abortion clinics along the borders of states where the procedure has been banned. In 2019, Planned Parenthood opened a large clinic in abortion-friendly Illinois, right along the border of Missouri (which had some of the nation's strictest abortion laws) in anticipation of *Roe* being overturned.[2] As of this writing, the FDA is looking to loosen restrictions on women's ability to receive abortion pills through the mail to make abortion "more accessible."[3]

In response to the Supreme Court's ruling, the pro-choice community has come out in full force, actively looking for ways to make access to chemical and surgical abortions faster, easier, and more convenient. Likewise, they have intentionally amplified messages that tend to resonate with Black women. For example, by emphasizing the maternal mortality crisis among Black women, they hope to convince already vulnerable women that banning abortion will lead to more deaths.[4]

Radio host Gloria Purvis adeptly rejects this faulty reasoning by articulating what these women say they actually want and need: "access to wholesome food and clean water, safe and affordable housing, good schools, good jobs, [and] spouses with good jobs." Purvis further explains, "The very women being used as mascots for abortion rights are the women who do not want abortion. The overemphasis on abortion while ignoring what these women want and need is reproductive coercion. The failure to meet their actual material needs while eagerly providing abortion does not provide what poor Black women and their families need. Their conditions will never improve by removing the unborn children from the community instead of removing the substandard conditions from the community."[5] This means the pro-life community must answer the question, How are *we* going to step up? What life-giving options will we provide to women facing unplanned pregnancies? How will we make choosing life easier and more accessible? Most importantly, how will we embrace a new mission? How will we fight for justice, disrupting the pathways that lead to abortion in the first place and slaying this evil at the source?

When you consider the entire landscape, it can be easy to feel overwhelmed. After all, we are talking about undoing more than a century's worth of prejudice, injustice, and social and financial inequity, not to mention trying to prevent nearly a million abortions from happening every year.[6] It's no wonder so many people throw up their hands in frustration and ask, "What can I possibly do?"

Well, for starters, we know that the majority of women seeking an abortion say they would prefer to parent if their circumstances were different,[7] the biggest obstacles being a lack of support from the father or other family members, lack of employment (or fear that having a child will result in job loss), lack of financial and material support, and lack of affordable housing. That means if we truly value life, we must find a way to meet these needs.

How do we do that? By using the gifts God has already given us.

TIME, TALENT, AND TREASURE

In Matthew 25, Jesus tells the story of a man who, before setting out on a journey, entrusted three of his servants with a portion of his fortune to steward in his absence.

He gave the first servant five bags of silver, he gave the second two bags, and he gave the third one bag.

As soon as the master left on his journey, the servant who was given five bags of silver invested them and earned five more. Likewise, the servant who was given two bags earned two more. But instead of investing his portion, the servant with the single bag of silver dug a hole in the ground and hid his master's money.

Eventually the master returned to see how his servants had managed the funds he had given them. The servant who had received five bags joyfully produced five more. The second servant revealed that he, too, had doubled the master's investment. The master was thrilled, telling both men, "Well done, my good and faithful servant."

But when the third servant handed the master the same bag of silver he had originally been given, the master was angry. "You wicked and lazy servant!" he shouted. "Why didn't you deposit my money in the bank? At least I could have gotten some interest on it." Then he told his other servants, "Take the money from this servant, give it to the one with the ten bags of silver, and throw this useless servant into outer darkness" (see Matthew 25:14-30).

Jesus has given all of us gifts of time, talent, and treasure to steward for his Kingdom. As we enter this post-*Roe* era, it is incumbent on all of us who value life to be good and faithful servants of these gifts by finding ways to invest them.

Take my parents, for instance. I recently called them for our weekly check-in. After the phone rang a few times, my mom picked up.

"Hey, Mommy!" I said in my usual greeting.

"Well, hello, Benjamin. How are you?"

"I'm good, Mommy," I said. "I'm doing good." But before I had the chance to ask how she was feeling and how her morning walk had gone, I heard a familiar yet unexpected sound in the background.

Is that a baby crying? I wondered. None of her grandchildren were local. Besides, only two of them were even remotely young enough to be making the types of gurgling baby noises I heard. "Mommy," I said. "Whose baby is that?"

My mother laughed and explained that a woman in their church had been contemplating an abortion. The mother's situation was less than ideal: her marriage was on the brink of collapse. She and her husband already had a child, and he didn't want another. Still, my parents and others in the church compassionately counseled her to bring her pregnancy to term.

This was not a matter of convincing her that her child had value, mind you. She held strong convictions about the inherent dignity and worth of life from conception. However, the lack of support from her husband, the economic strain, and the fear of being unable to adequately care for another child—potentially as a single mom—felt overwhelming. But with the encouragement and care of my parents and others in the church community, she made the decision to bring her baby boy into the world.

It wasn't just the affirmation from her spiritual family that made the prospect of mothering two children on her own feel doable, however; it was their commitment to walk beside her and help her as she ventured into the unknown.

"I told her I would watch him a few times a week," my mother explained. "Especially when she's at work or when she needs to pick up her other child."

I fell silent for a moment. It's not that I wouldn't expect such commitment from my parents. They have always been extremely generous people. But in that moment, it hit me that this is what it looks like to walk out the intentions so many of us in the pro-life movement talk about when it comes to loving both woman and child.

When my father got on the phone, he explained their involvement as only he could. "Son," he said, "how could we continue to encourage her to have her baby if we were unwilling to tangibly help her parent him once he got here?"

That's what it's all about. Protecting the baby in the womb from extermination is a vital part of what it means to be pro-life, but it's just the beginning. Being truly committed to life also means doing everything we can to ensure that these babies—and their mothers—not only survive but thrive.

That may mean helping an expectant mother purchase the diapers, formula, clothing, and other supplies she needs; buying her children birthday and Christmas gifts; donating a seldom-used car so she can have transportation to and from work; or cosigning a lease on an apartment so she can have a safe place to live. It may mean providing counseling or legal advice, offering medical services to her and her family, tutoring her so she can finish school, or helping her find a job. Or it might mean providing a ride to work, doctor visits, or the grocery store. For my parents, it means giving the gift of free childcare so the mother can work to provide for her children.

The point is, we all have something we can give, whether it's time, money, or a skill set. As life-affirming Christians, our challenge—indeed, our obligation—is to use our God-given gifts to help those in need.

I was (and still am) humbled by my parents' willingness to stand in the gap for this young woman—not just with their words but with their deeds. As I write this, that baby is about a year and a half old, and they are still standing in that gap, opening their home, sacrificing their time, and walking beside that mom. That's what being pro-life looks like in a post-*Roe* world—and that's what being a faithful Christian looks like *always*.

WALKING IT OUT

While Scripture is clear that we are saved through faith in Christ alone, James also teaches that the evidence of faith is good works.

What good is it, dear brothers and sisters, if you say you have faith but don't show it by your actions? Can that kind of faith save anyone? Suppose you see a brother or sister who has no food or clothing, and you say, "Good-bye and have a good day; stay warm and eat well"—but then you don't give that person any food or clothing. What good does that do? So you see, faith by itself isn't enough. Unless it produces good deeds, it is dead and useless. Just as the body is dead without breath, so also faith is dead without good works.

JAMES 2:14-17, 26

To be abundantly clear, James is not saying we are saved by our works. On the contrary, he is saying that our works are a natural by-product of our faith. Likewise, our pro-life commitment should produce pro-life fruit. Dr. Tony Evans puts it this way: "Faith is measured by your feet."[8]

There are myriad ways in which we, as individuals in the pro-life arena, can walk out our faith.

Foster or Adopt

My friend DJ and his wife, Glorya, have a heart for vulnerable children. DJ's parents were teenagers when they became pregnant, and both came from poor families. But they were committed to having their baby, so they married and went on to raise six children.

Inspired by his parents' commitment to life, DJ and his wife began volunteering at a crisis pregnancy center in 2010, helping young couples who were dealing with unplanned pregnancies. After encouraging multiple couples to consider adoption as an alternative to abortion, DJ and Glorya—who already had three sons of their own—decided to look into adoption and foster care themselves.

"One day as my wife and I were talking . . . here we were telling all these other people about adoption, [and we thought] . . . maybe we should look into this adoption or foster care thing," said DJ. "So we did. We did research."[9]

One evening they went to an informational meeting at church, and after learning more about the foster care crisis in the US, they sensed God calling them to get involved. "The question for us transitioned to *Should we . . . be a part of the solution?*"

They started training to become foster parents, and after fostering several children short-term, they adopted their youngest daughter in 2013. Since then, they've remained engaged in the foster care community, coming alongside other families who are going through the fostering process and speaking at churches to inspire others to get involved.

In 2019, following the passage of New York's Reproductive Health Act, which expanded abortion rights, decriminalized abortion, and eliminated several restrictions on abortion, a young couple from Radford, Virginia, stepped into action. Blake and Sarah Thomas posted a photo of themselves on Facebook. In it, they held a poster that read "Please don't abort. We will adopt your baby!" The post quickly went viral, and within a week, they had been contacted by dozens of expectant mothers, many of whom, after speaking with the Thomases, decided to keep their babies or actively pursue adoption.

"I'm Facebook friends with many of the mothers [who] contacted me back in January," Sarah says. "My Facebook is covered with baby pictures right now, which makes me so happy!"[10] The Thomases have since adopted a baby from foster care and, as of this writing, are in the process of adopting another little boy.

Perhaps your calling is to adopt a child who has been rescued from abortion. Or maybe God is calling you to be a foster parent for children who desperately need a loving parent. Or perhaps your role is simply to provide emotional or material support for couples who feel called to foster or adopt. Regardless of the way they come into our lives, all babies require time, talent, and treasure to thrive. As the father of seven, I can assure you that very few parents refuse a willing and helping hand.

DJ, Glorya, Sarah, and Blake didn't just talk about making a difference; they put their money where their mouth was and got involved. Now, I realize adoption and foster care aren't for everyone, and if that's not your particular calling, there's nothing wrong with that. That's why 1 Corinthians 12 reminds us that the body has many different parts. But if we're going to make abortion unthinkable and unnecessary, at some point, in some capacity, we *all* need to get some skin in the game.

Be the "R" for a PRC

A few years ago, I was at a fundraising banquet for a pregnancy resource center (PRC) in Greensboro, North Carolina. I was seated by a young woman who worked as a social media influencer. As we got to talking, I learned that she was really into online platforms such as Facebook, TikTok, Instagram, YouTube, and Twitter, and the PRC had hired her to help develop and expand their social media reach. It's something she loves to do, and frankly, she understands it better than a lot of us older folks do. Now she uses that talent to create and promote informational videos about protecting life.

At present, there are more than 2,700 PRCs across the nation that empower abortion-determined women to choose life.[11] Many of them also assist with health care, employment, housing, and the Supplemental Nutrition Assistance Program (SNAP). In addition to providing tangible services, they also provide counseling, emotional support, and hope. While some of these organizations receive state funding, others—especially those that are faith-based—are hesitant to accept public funding because of the protocols and procedures that accompany such assistance. Whether these PRCs are publicly or privately funded, the employees and volunteers work tirelessly to meet the needs of the women who come through their doors. And these agencies *always* need support.

Consider reaching out to your local PRC and asking how you can help. If you have the means, you might provide ongoing financial support to help cover staff salaries and daily expenditures, or you might make a one-time donation toward a big-ticket item such as an ultrasound machine. If you can't afford something like that on your own, you might take up a collection at work, at church, or in your neighborhood. You can also collect and donate new or gently used clothing, toys, cribs, changing tables, strollers, high chairs, and car seats. Offer to help out at fundraisers and events, or volunteer to spend a few hours a week answering phones, doing clerical work, or providing tech support. If you have a background in counseling, you might consider ministering to young men and women struggling in the wake of an abortion, or you might host or facilitate a support group.

Whatever your gifts or abilities, I promise you, there's a way to use them in support of life. "The harvest is great, but the workers are few." Be a worker.

Share Your Story

Sometimes we don't want to share our personal stories because we still are dealing with our own trauma. But sharing your testimony may be the most powerful gift you can give someone who is struggling with the same fears and disappointments you've experienced. Nobody wants to feel alone.

Sadly, nearly one in four women in the United States (23.7 percent) will have an abortion by age forty-five.[12] That's a lot of collective trauma. For those who are willing to share their experiences, those numbers also represent a lot of much-needed empathy and support.

I was at a fundraising banquet for a PRC network in Chicago when Meagan shared her story. She was seventeen when she found out she was pregnant. Devastated and ashamed, she was afraid her family would be disappointed in her, and she ended up having an abortion.

"I don't remember much about the day," she said. "But I do remember after the abortion being put in a room to rest . . . and there was one girl who kept screaming and crying that she wanted her baby. And I remember having the thought, *That's what I should have done. . . .* That was the end of my life as I knew it. I was never the same again." When Meagan got married, she told her husband about the abortion, but she didn't share all she'd gone through. "I think he got a glimpse of it when one day, we're at the park. . . . I hear these teenagers laughing and I start crying. He says, 'What's wrong?' and I said, 'I can't take it anymore. I can't take it. I hear people laughing or whispering, and I think, *They can see it on me. They can see that I've had an abortion, and that's what they're talking about.'* And he just said to me, 'You need help.' . . . I never thought I needed help. I thought I was living out the consequences of my sins. . . . And about that time, someone told me the true meaning of the Cross. . . . So at thirty-six, I asked for forgiveness, and I knew he had forgiven me. That was the beginning of a new life."

The number one thing Satan would have people like Meagan do is be quiet and not talk about their experiences. Research indicates that post-abortive women are at a highly increased risk for clinical depression, alcohol and drug abuse, suicidal thoughts, post-traumatic stress disorder, and other emotional and mental health issues.[13] But there is power in sharing our testimonies with others who are dealing with the same sort of trauma and grief. For many, simply knowing they are not alone is a blessing in itself. Some, like Meagan, will find forgiveness in Christ during the recovery process, which is the greatest gift we can receive. Now Meagan is sharing that same message of hope with others.

Remember, being pro-life isn't just about advocating for babies in the womb; it's also about meeting the physical, emotional, and spiritual needs of everyone involved—both those contemplating abortion and those suffering in its wake.

Pray

Christian author and pro-life activist Randy Alcorn recently wrote, "As should be obvious from the intensity of the outcries to the Supreme Court decision overturning *Roe v. Wade*, when it comes to abortion, we are not talking about a topic that is just hotter than any other. Abortion is birthed by a force of darkness that will bitterly resist every effort to combat it, and which requires earnest and sustained prayer."[14]

In many respects, we are in the spiritual battle of our lives, and there is no greater power in spiritual warfare than prayer. All too often, we sell prayer short, not believing it will make any discernible difference. But movements of God happen when people pray, because when we pray, God moves us. When we seek his face, he informs our feet.

Commit yourself to prayer. Ask God to show you how he can best use your time, talent, and treasure in the fight for life, and then be open to his leading.

Pray for an end to abortion. Pray for justice—for the preborn, the marginalized, and the disenfranchised. Pray for equality. Pray for the young men and women trembling in the face of an unplanned pregnancy. Pray that they will find the emotional, financial, and spiritual support they need to choose life. Pray for those who have already suffered an abortion, that they will find peace and forgiveness.

Pray for those working in PRCs, ministering to young men and women at the most critical juncture of their lives. Pray that God will give the volunteers and staff the strength, patience, and wisdom to convince those in their care to choose life.

Pray for the children in foster care, that they will find loving, nurturing homes where they can flourish. And pray for those considering adoption, that they will find the encouragement and support they need to open their homes to those who have none. Pray for the grandparents and empty nesters who have made the commitment to stand in the gap and provide real, tangible support for young mothers so they can work to give their children a better life.

Pray for our elected representatives, that they will have the wisdom and courage to create laws and programs to preserve and promote life in every stage and every condition. Pray for legal and social redress, that this nation will act on behalf of broken people and communities so they will be made whole. Pray for parents as they humbly teach their children the value of life and the importance of upholding human dignity.

In other words, "Pray without ceasing" (1 Thessalonians 5:17, ESV).

And one other thing.

CAST YOUR BALLOT

Second to prayer, I believe the single greatest weapon we have in our arsenal as we engage in this new fight for life is our vote. Former congressman John Lewis, the late civil rights leader and member of the Georgia House of Representatives, said, "The vote is precious. It is the most powerful nonviolent tool we have in a democratic society, and we must use it."[15] I agree wholeheartedly.

The right to vote is a hallmark of American society, one that has been secured and retained through blood sacrifice. It is not to be taken lightly, especially for Black Americans. I am often reminded that it took multiple civil rights acts and constitutional amendments to grant women and descendants of the enslaved the right to have their voices heard. So if not for my own sake but for the sake of those who were denied, beaten, and even murdered, I take voting very seriously and believe everyone should engage in this process.

Yet as important as voting is, it can be a frustrating experience, especially given our highly polarized political system, which thrives on extremes. Election season can be particularly difficult for Christians because no political party or candidate represents the fullness of God's Kingdom, and none of the initiatives or referenda proposed by politicians represent the full revelation God has given us about justice, righteousness, grace, truth, mercy, and love.

In fact, the gospel flies directly in the face of our political extremes. In Scripture, we see a God who is both holy and just. We see a God who both shows mercy and provides correction. And we see a God who is full of both grace and truth. Throughout Scripture—and in the person of Jesus—we see these apparent contradictions. This divine amalgamation of both/and stands in stark contrast to a two-party system that forces us to choose either/or: conservative or liberal, pro-life or pro-choice, government-funded health care or privatized health care, social responsibility or individual rights.

As believers, we are called to think beyond our bifurcated political system and consider the more complex nature of these issues. Abortion, for example, is a particularly complicated issue. One Christian might reason that the Bible is abundantly clear about the sanctity of life. The fact that God formed us in our mothers' wombs means that all human beings have inherent value and dignity, regardless of their stage of development. With this in mind, they cast their vote accordingly. Another Christian might vote for a candidate whose socioeconomic policies they believe will better serve marginalized women and children by creating a more sustainable path to human flourishing.

The problem isn't with the reasoning of either voter but with a two-party system that often forces us to choose between protecting a human life *before* birth and providing a safe, healthy, and hopeful environment for that child to thrive *after* they're born. As political strategist Justin Giboney writes, "One side often neglects the tough situations women face, while the other elevates personal choice over human dignity."[16]

The truth is, there are no absolutes in this political equation. As a result, we need to extend grace to our brothers and sisters in Christ when discussing the issues they prioritize in voting. No matter which candidate we vote for, we must be mindful that there are believers on both sides of the debate and not use the ballot box as a litmus test for who is a Christian and who is not.

Furthermore, casting our ballot should not be the end of the equation. Civic engagement means encouraging elected Democrats to push their party toward recognizing the personhood and dignity of every human being, while urging Republicans to push their party to repair social and economic injustices. We need to recognize that no party, including Independents, has a stronghold on these issues and that within each party are men and women who hold more nuanced viewpoints than those of the party's broader platform.

Take my friend Katrina Jackson, for instance. Katrina is a state senator in Louisiana who is passionate about protecting the preborn. As an attorney, she has written and introduced several pieces of legislation aimed at protecting and preserving life—most notably, the Love Life Amendment, which removed wording guaranteeing the right to an abortion from the Louisiana Constitution.[17] What I love about Katrina is that in a landscape dominated by extremes, she is both a card-carrying Democrat and a passionate pro-lifer who has made it her mission to reach across party lines and encourage Democrats, Republicans, and Independents to work together to eliminate the need for abortion.

"Protecting life is an issue that's paramount and is not about party lines," says Jackson. "Because life is not a party issue."[18] Jackson affirms, "I don't care if you are Black or white, Democrat or Republican, male or female . . . everyone has something to contribute to the common goal of saving babies."[19] She continues, "I think that we definitely have to still participate and focus on the law, but we have to do more to engage the general public . . . and educate the community about why being pro-life is so important."[20]

She's not wrong. As it happens, I am working on this chapter on the eve of midterm elections. As I look at my sample ballot, I see options for the United States Senate, governor, lieutenant governor, secretary of state, attorney general, commissioner of agriculture, school superintendent, commissioner of labor, county commissioner, and soil and water conservation district supervisor. While I recognized some names right away, others were completely unfamiliar to me. To be honest, I wasn't even sure what some of these lesser-known offices are or what they do, let alone which candidates are likely to do a better job of serving in these positions until I looked them up.

As voters, we need to make sure we're educated. I'm not saying you have to become an expert, but I do believe there is power in understanding the bigger political picture and where you fit in.

In 2018, several of my teammates from the New Orleans Saints and I attended a daylong discovery meeting with the Orleans Public Defenders. Chief defender Derwyn Bunton led the conversation, explaining that 85 percent of people who go through the criminal justice system in Louisiana need a public defender. While they should be presumed innocent, nearly two-thirds remain in jail before trial simply because they can't afford their bond. Far too often, as Bryan Stevenson says, "The opposite of poverty is not wealth; the opposite of poverty is justice."[21]

I remember sitting in the viewing seats in the Orleans Parish Criminal District Court later that day, my first time witnessing bail hearings. As men and women clad in orange stood before the judge, I wondered not just about their guilt and innocence but about how their economic status would impact their ability to retain employment, parent their children, and pay rent prior to their trial. In a siloed world, I'd never considered this glaring injustice, largely because I hadn't had to.

Sometimes learning doesn't happen organically—it must be intentional. We only know our own experiences and what we've been taught. The world we live in is the result of a complex web of current and historical people, policies, and programs. If we want to have a grasp on the present, we need to hunger for the hows and whys outside our immediate spheres.

Pro-lifers would benefit by staying abreast of developments in maternal health care and legislative efforts that protect preborn life. In the same way, they should engage with voices and materials that paint a more complete picture of the obstacles these women face in making a more just society. Comprehending causal links will not occur spontaneously; it requires diligent work.

Throughout history, God has used his people to carry out his mission, and right now is our time in history. As his ambassadors on earth, we must educate ourselves on both injustices that happened in the past and those happening right before our eyes. Only then can we vote with integrity and use our influence to fight for the oppressed, the vulnerable, and the hopeless. Only then can we stand for good and relentlessly advocate for kindness and justice.

Vote, and encourage others to do the same. Educate yourself on the candidates and the issues, and carefully and prayerfully consider which boxes, if checked, will have the greatest impact on life and justice—bearing in mind that abortion is not the only issue at play in the fight for life.

Education, housing reform, minimum wage, workers' rights, health care, subsidized housing, infrastructure, clean air and water, transportation, taxes, and government-funded programs are also necessary to flourishing, and if we are truly committed to advocating for life and justice from the womb to the tomb, we need to take the whole landscape into consideration and cast our ballots accordingly.

And if you aren't satisfied with the way things are, consider running for office yourself. Several years ago, Lucy McBath, a flight attendant in Georgia, lost her seventeen-year-old son, Jordan, to gun violence. He was sitting in a car with his friends at a gas station listening to the radio when a white man approached, confronted the boys about the volume, and then shot Jordan three times.

"I felt like in that moment that everything I had done to protect him, it wasn't good enough," said McBath. "Everything I had thought I had done, putting him in the right community and putting him in the right schools and keeping him around the right kids, the right families, it didn't matter because he was a young Black male, and it was simply because of the color of his skin."[22]

Feeling the need to do something, McBath got involved with Moms Demand Action for Gun Sense in America and eventually became the national spokeswoman. Then, in 2018, incensed by the Marjory Stoneman Douglas High School shooting in Parkland, Florida, she decided to run for Congress so she could help pass stronger gun control laws. She won—and she did.

McBath wasn't a career politician, nor did she ever plan on being one. She was just a mom who wanted to spare other mothers from experiencing the same grief she'd experienced. "I never expected this to happen," she admits. "But . . . in light of all my experiences, to not do anything is a tragedy in itself."[23] McBath says, "I was raised that you fight to protect and care for the people that you can believe in and that you love. You fight for your community. You fight for those that feel defenseless."[24]

Now, I'm not saying you have to run for Congress to

make an impact. In fact, much of what happens in the daily lives of Americans is decided on the local level. Decisions like bringing grocery stores into inner-city areas, improving public transit, and bringing more resources to at-risk communities often happen at city and county levels. You could run for your local school board and create policies that improve student retention, implement after-school programs, or lobby for a more inclusive curriculum.

Making abortion unthinkable and unnecessary will take a concerted effort from life-supporting individuals and organizations from all backgrounds—Christians and those from other religious backgrounds, wealthy and blue-collar, Boomers and Gen Zers, Black and white, and yes, Republicans and Democrats.

We may express our convictions differently and have different ideas about the best way to accomplish our common goals, but there are life-affirming people voting, advocating, and serving all across the political spectrum. We need to lower our defenses and engage with those whose lifestyles and beliefs look different from ours and start focusing not on what separates us but on what unites us.

GOLIATH IS GONE

Roe may have been overturned, but the fight isn't over. On the contrary, it has intensified. In many respects, the new fight for life is even harder, because there's no longer a giant standing on the other side of the valley.

For fifty years, *Roe*, like Goliath, has been the common enemy that pro-life activists have sought to defeat. And while the giant may have fallen, the same obstacles that stand in the way of abortion-determined women choosing life are still there. There are still unplanned pregnancies. There are still thousands of young women in need of financial, emotional, and spiritual support. There is still a sizable wage gap. There are still educational disparities. There is still poverty. And there is still a two-party system that makes it exceptionally difficult to legislate and address these issues holistically.

The celebration is over. The confetti has fallen, and the cheering crowds have gone home. But there is still work to be done. And this work isn't flashy. Much of it happens in obscurity—as it does for my parents, who babysit for a young mother so she can go to work. Or for DJ and Glorya, who provide foster care for children whose parents are unwilling or unable to care for them. Or for the social media influencer I met, who creates videos for her local pregnancy resource center. Or for the school board member, who fights to improve student retention and graduation rates in impoverished districts.

People love headlines, but there are no headlines or front-page stories recognizing this type of work. That's why the battles before us now are even harder: there's no earthly glory at stake. But for those who commit themselves to doing this work—advocating, ministering, serving, loving, and caring—our Father, who sees everything, will reward them (see Matthew 6:3).

THE POWER OF ONE

According to the familiar legend,[25] there was an old man who had a habit of taking early-morning walks on the beach. One morning when he was walking, he saw a shadowy figure in the distance that looked like a girl dancing. He walked up to her, and when he got closer, he realized that she wasn't dancing; she was picking up starfish and throwing them into the ocean, one by one.

The old man asked her, "What are you doing?"

She bent down and picked up another starfish. "The sun is coming up and the tide is going out. If I don't throw them back in, they'll die."

"But young lady," he said, "you do realize that there are miles and miles of shoreline, and probably thousands of starfish all over this beach. You can't possibly make a difference."

She listened politely and then paused, picked up a starfish, and threw it into the ocean. "Well . . . I made a difference for that one."

The old man looked at her and thought about what she'd said. Inspired, he bent down beside her and started throwing starfish into the sea. Soon other people who were walking by stopped to inquire about what they were doing. Eventually hundreds of people were throwing starfish into the sea.

They probably didn't get to all the starfish. As a matter of fact, there's no way they could have. Despite their best efforts, millions of those starfish dried up in the sun and died—but not before one saved starfish turned into hundreds, and hundreds turned into thousands. In her own way, that one young woman rescued countless thousands of starfish, just by doing what she could.

I can't promise that abortion is going to go away completely in our lifetime. But I can promise that the investment, time, and energy you put into the effort will not be in vain. Countless children, mothers, and families will be saved through your intentional action.

You'll never know how contagious your actions can be. You'll never know if your obedience and your voice will reach someone at the tipping point—someone who needs just one more word of encouragement to do the right thing.

So don't give up.

Keep moving forward.

Pick up a starfish and throw it into the sea.

If only for that one, you *can* make a difference.

CHAPTER 6

THE ROOT OF THE PROBLEM

Folks don't want to get to the why. . . . Folks don't want to deal with what's happening economically, don't want to deal with what's happening with lack of opportunity in terms of lack of resources. . . . And you have to deal with that.

ROLAND MARTIN, CEO OF BLACK STAR NETWORK

Sometimes people accuse me of being overly concerned with the past. When I speak publicly on the sanctity of human life inside the womb, white, religious, pro-life conservatives applaud. But when I speak on the sanctity of human life *outside* the womb—specifically Black life—they can be less than kind, and—in some cases—downright racist.

Here are some common responses I get after speaking or posting about the value of life for all people: "What about Black-on-Black crime?" "But you're a millionaire," "We fought a war to end slavery," "You people need to forgive and stop complaining," or "Stop being so woke" (even if they don't know what *woke* means). I've learned to keep scrolling and not allow the keyboard warriors to drag me down, knowing that these comments reveal an ignorance that makes it difficult to achieve the "just society" espoused by American tropes.

Dr. Martin Luther King Jr. wrote, "Many of the ugly pages of American history have been obscured and forgotten. A society is always eager to cover misdeeds with a cloak of forgetfulness, but no society can fully repress an ugly past when the ravages persist into the present. America owes a debt of justice which it has only begun to pay."[1]

When I consider the women who are having abortions (the majority of whom are Black), I simply cannot divorce the injustices of the past from those that are still unrecognized today—injustices that, if not addressed, will appall generations tomorrow.

We like simple action steps that will solve a problem quickly. We expect that if we drop a coin into the slot and push A7, our favorite snack will automatically drop into the receptacle below, and our hunger will be assuaged. Unfortunately, most of life's issues are neither quickly nor easily resolved. Even when they could be, we too often lack the will and the moral integrity to carry through because the solution will cost us more than we're willing to pay. As King went on to say, "The great majority of Americans are suspended between these opposing attitudes. They are uneasy with injustice but unwilling yet to pay a significant price to eradicate it."[2]

The pursuit of justice is most often a messy one, presenting challenges that are simultaneously simple and difficult. But make no mistake: a true pro-life commitment to justice will require an intentional, strategic, precise effort to make right what has been wrong. It will require personal sacrifice. And it may take decades to achieve. The question is, Where should we begin?

Over the course of my NFL career, I dealt with numerous ankle, knee, and Achilles injuries. Even though I'm no longer playing, my knee in particular gives me trouble from time to time. One of the things I learned from my physical therapist is that when my knee hurts, it's usually because, in addition to all the scar tissue, my hips are off. So in addition to addressing the immediate symptoms with ice and Advil, I also address the underlying structural problems in the kinetic chain. Because while a pain reliever will alleviate the ache for a while, if the problem is being caused by the misalignment of my hips, it will just keep coming back.

Similarly, when it comes to abortion, we tend to address the symptoms instead of looking at the root cause. And while it's important to provide women with immediate material assistance such as diapers, formula, and clothes, until we eradicate the driving factors that lead to abortion in the first place, the problem will continue, with or without abortion providers.

The following proposed solutions—while by no means exhaustive—are directed primarily at concerns that need to be addressed at a societal level. While these may seem like large-scale problems that are beyond the scope of our influence, the reality is that we need to think about ways our society can and should change. If we don't change our assumptions and the status quo, we will continue in the same rut, battling the same societal ailments—but with increasingly dire consequences.

SEED MONEY

After the Civil War ended in 1865, four million formerly enslaved Americans owned approximately .5 percent of the national wealth. More than 150 years later, Black Americans hold only about 3 percent of the nation's wealth.[3] While some Black individuals and communities have enjoyed a measure of economic success and political influence (and subsequently have been held up by some as evidence of an equal playing field in our society), the larger picture is vastly different.

In Boston, for example, in 2015 the median net worth of a white family was $247,500. The median net worth of a Black family was close to zero.[4] We also know that a Black child is nearly three times more likely to be born into poverty than a white child.[5] When you're born into poverty, it's simply harder to escape it.

Decades of institutional racism and discriminatory policies such as redlining and segregation have systematically denied Black communities the rights and access to building generational wealth. And it's not just the millions of dollars in wages that were denied to enslaved descendants that have set the Black community behind. It's also the millions in restricted wages and cumulative social penalties that have been levied upon them all the way through the twentieth century and into today's labor market. And if Congress's lackluster response to H.R.40 (a bill that established a commission to study and develop remedies for past and present discrimination for American descendants of the enslaved) is any indicator, odds seem to be against the approval of any such reparations.

Without a radical solution, America will continue to be home to one of the worst rates of income inequality of any wealthy nation. What most people don't realize, however, is that a possible solution already exists.

In 1967, Dr. Martin Luther King Jr. wrote that government aid programs all have a "common failing—they are indirect. Each seeks to solve poverty by first solving something else. I am now convinced that the simplest approach will prove to be the most effective—the solution to poverty is to abolish it directly by a now widely discussed measure: the guaranteed income."[6]

Guaranteed income is not a new concept. Thomas Paine was one of the first to introduce the idea in the West way back in 1797. The idea that God had ordained some to wretched misery and some to opulent luxury turned Paine's stomach. "It is wrong to say God made rich and poor," Paine argued. "He made only male and female." Thus, Paine proposed what we now refer to as a universal basic income, essentially providing all citizens with a set monthly stipend—no strings attached—which would effectively address and eliminate poverty at its source.[7]

And it works.

In January of 2019, the Stockton Economic Empowerment Demonstration (SEED) in Stockton, California, provided five hundred dollars a month to 125 of the city's poorest residents for twenty-four months. While skeptics feared that recipients would spend the money on drugs, alcohol, or non-essential luxury items and either quit their jobs or not look for work, studies found that SEED participants were twice as likely to find full-time work as nonparticipants. In addition, the majority of their stipend was spent on food, utility bills, gas, and car maintenance. Participants also showed overall improvements in mental and physical health.[8]

Likewise, a study led by Nobel Prize–winning development economist Abhijit Banerjee concluded that the distribution of unconditional cash in low-income countries had positive effects on "income, assets, savings, borrowing, total expenditure, food expenditure, dietary diversity, school attendance, test scores, cognitive development, use of health facilities, labor force participation, child labor migration, domestic violence, women's empowerment, marriage, fertility, and use of contraception, among others."[9]

A similar program is currently underway in Jackson, Mississippi, where Magnolia Mother's Trust provides Black mothers living in poverty with $1,000 per month for a year—no strings attached. Dr. Aisha Nyandoro, who founded the program, says the goal is "to change how our society talks about Black women and poverty—that it's not a personal failing. That there are systemic barriers that allow Black women to be the most vulnerable financially, even though they are the most highly invested in the labor market."[10]

And just like in Stockton, it's working. According to the organization's report, "82 percent of the women who participated felt more hopeful about their children's futures; 79 percent felt more hopeful about their own futures; and 76.2 percent reported that with money from the Magnolia Mother's Trust, they were able to take their children on trips, pay for extracurricular activities and afford school supplies."[11]

In response to the pandemic, President Biden signed a dramatically expanded version of the child tax credit, giving parents $3,600 per child per year—essentially a small guaranteed income—reducing the child poverty rate by nearly 30 percent. "Scholars called it one of the most important moves to fight poverty since the creation of Social Security."[12]

This type of program is not a handout; it is a hand up. As Nelson Mandela said, "Overcoming poverty is not a gesture of charity. It is an act of justice. It is the protection of a fundamental human right, the right to dignity and a decent life."[13]

Some people view governmental programs like these as being affiliated with one political party. They may object to increased governmental involvement and argue that this kind of assistance is better handled by churches and nonprofit organizations. But the reality is, the kind of justice that results in action requires the buy-in of an entire society—from churches to nonprofits to government agencies to individuals.

Of course, the biggest objection to guaranteed-income programs is the cost. If the government provided $1,000 a month to every American, it would come out to roughly $3.1 trillion a year. However, studies have shown that income inequality has a direct correlation to things like crime rates, drug abuse, incarceration, domestic violence, and physical and mental health, which ultimately cost billions of tax dollars. Researchers have found that it would actually be cheaper to provide free homes to people without a house than to absorb the various costs associated with homelessness.[14]

The bottom line is that King was correct: the shortest distance between two points is a straight line. When it comes to a controversial initiative such as guaranteed income, there is always room for debate about the most effective approach.

But the new fight for life is one that considers how to provide immediate, direct support to mothers, children, and families in their moments of need while simultaneously enacting structural change. And while guaranteed income might seem like a revolutionary concept, Scripture describes a similar method of God-ordained care for his chosen people, with principles that we would be wise to emulate.

JUBILANT JUSTICE

Buried in the book of Leviticus, amid a seemingly endless catalog of laws and restrictions, is one of the most radical proposals for eliminating poverty in all of human history.

After laying out the instructions for the proper way to worship and make sacrifices, God turns his attention to teaching the Israelites how to live their lives in a way that sets them apart from everyone else. While some Old Testament laws have been fulfilled in the coming of Jesus, the underlying principles about the just treatment of fellow human beings still hold true. Leviticus 25:8-10 says,

> Count off seven Sabbath years, seven sets of seven years, adding up to forty-nine years in all. Then on the Day of Atonement in the fiftieth year, blow the ram's horn loud and long throughout the land. Set this year apart as holy, a time to proclaim freedom throughout the land for all who live there. It will be a jubilee year for you, when each of you may return to the land that belonged to your ancestors and return to your own clan.

In other words, every fifty years, all debts would be canceled, all slaves would be set free, and all land would be returned to its original owners.

That meant that if an Israelite fell on hard times due to sickness or injury, he was no longer able to provide for himself and his family, and he had to sell his land and work for someone else to survive, God arranged for a way out. Once every generation, those who were struggling would get an automatic do-over of sorts. There would always be rich people and poor people, but God's will was that no one group would ever be locked into generational wealth or poverty. He wanted them to rely solely on him for provision rather than on what they owned, which would turn their hearts from him as the ultimate provider. God also wanted his people to treat one another with the kind of dignity and respect that would set them apart from other nations.

While the Jubilee represents a spiritual reset, God also ingrained his civil law into the culture for their own preservation and moral order. The concept of reparation is rooted in Scripture to address humankind's inevitable sinfulness toward one another.[15] God provides many laws that protect the vulnerable and prescribe personal responsibility for wrongdoing. Earlier in Leviticus, God gives the instruction that anyone who steals from another must "make restitution by paying the full price plus an additional 20 percent to the person [they] have harmed" (Leviticus 6:5).

Exodus 22 says, "If an animal is grazing in a field or vineyard and the owner lets it stray into someone else's field to graze, then the animal's owner must pay compensation from the best of his own grain or grapes." It goes on to say, "If you are burning thornbushes and the fire gets out of control and spreads into another person's field, destroying the sheaves or the uncut grain or the whole crop, the one who started the fire must pay for the lost crop" (verses 5-6).

In the New Testament, Luke tells the story of Zacchaeus, a tax collector, who upon meeting Jesus not only gave half of his money to the poor but paid back those he'd cheated four times what he owed them (see Luke 19:8).

After the Babylonians burned down the city of Jerusalem, destroyed the Temple, and sent the Israelites into exile, King Cyrus returned the Israelites to Jerusalem to rebuild the Temple. On top of that, he gave them back all the gold and silver that Nebuchadnezzar had taken. He instructed that anyone who encountered Israelites heading back to Jerusalem "contribute toward their expenses by giving them silver and gold, supplies for the journey, and livestock, as well as a voluntary offering for the Temple of God in Jerusalem" (Ezra 1:4). Mind you, this was two generations after the fact. Cyrus had not directly committed any crimes against the Israelites, nor had any of his people. But at the Lord's prompting, he still paid restitution to their descendants and fully restored them.

That's what real justice looks like.

REPAYING OUR EDUCATIONAL DEBT

A couple of years ago, I spoke at an event in Little Rock, Arkansas. Even though it was a quick in-and-out trip, I knew I had to make time to see Little Rock Central High School, where, in 1957, nine Black students attempted to attend their local school—an act that presented the first major test of the federal government's ability to enforce the 1954 *Brown v. Board of Education* Supreme Court ruling outlawing segregation in public schools.

On my way to the airport, I stopped in front of the school and stood in the crisp predawn air, imagining the deafening yells from the raging mob, hell-bent on preventing these children from exercising their right to an equal education. Though the children were initially turned away by armed National Guardsmen at the order of the governor, President Eisenhower deployed federal troops to usher these students to school several weeks later. Across the nation, the tumultuous, decades-long process of desegregation had only begun.

Today our nation's schools are still largely segregated, and this trend has increased in recent decades. A study of eighth graders revealed that only one in eight white students attend a school where the majority of students are Black or from another ethnic group, while seven in ten Black children attend public schools fitting that description.[16] It also showed that Black students are more likely to attend high-poverty schools with majority non-white students, whereas the likelihood of white children attending similar schools is under 10 percent.

This is not to say that the goal for any group is to attend school with the other (although many studies have proven the benefits of cross-cultural exposure). Nor is it to imply that white institutions are inherently better or more desirable. It is simply an observation that resources are not dispensed in an honorable or fair fashion. All-Black primary schools have raised future scholars, civil leaders, and savants, but they have done so with facilities, materials, and teacher salaries that are not on par with those of all-white schools. While wealthier districts offer students the latest in technology, robust extracurricular programs, and a wide array of electives, underfunded schools struggle to meet even the most basic student needs, making do with outdated technology, older textbooks, and fewer resources.

More often than not, school systems reflect the wealth of the neighborhoods they serve. When neighborhoods are segregated—not just ethnically, but socioeconomically— areas with predominantly Black populations are typically home to underfunded schools. But just as the color of a person's skin should not dictate the way they are treated, a student's zip code should not determine the quality of their education. Yet the intertwining of race and poverty continues to disadvantage Black children, resulting in what distinguished professor of urban education Gloria Ladson-Billings calls "the education debt."[17]

Nationwide, majority-non-white districts get $23 billion less in funding than majority-white districts every year, despite having the same number of students.[18] That gap translates to a lower-quality education for many Black students and other students of color. And as Verna Williams, dean of the University of Cincinnati College of Law, is quick to point out, "The implications of not being able to get an education . . . are linked to people's ability to support themselves, to support their families, to have healthy communities."[19]

And it's not just a question of funding. Black students, on average, perform below their white counterparts in academics—for a variety of reasons. "Some students living in poverty don't have access to the healthcare they need," says researcher Ary Amerikaner. "They might come to school without glasses and can't see the board. How are they going to learn? Some might come to school having experienced certain traumatic or adverse experiences and need a place to process that."[20]

Also, because most curricula and standardized tests are developed by white middle-class educators and reflect white middle-class norms and values, students of color are often marginalized, their intelligence and achievement measured by unfamiliar yardsticks.

Children's academic success is largely contingent on the involvement of their parents, usually a by-product of their parents' own educational opportunities. Children whose parents are themselves college educated and who place an emphasis on learning and reading have an advantage over children whose parents have not matriculated. One study has shown that 80 percent of children raised by parents with college degrees were actively encouraged to attend a four-year college, while only 29 percent of children raised by parents without degrees were encouraged to do so.[21]

So why does this matter? According to studies, the more educated a woman is, the less likely she is to find herself with an unplanned pregnancy.[22] The fact that most women seeking an abortion have little more than a high school diploma bears this out.[23] In general, women are not paid as much as men regardless of education level, and statistically Black women are paid the least, earning 35 percent less than white men with equal education.[24] So while many Black women are educated, that doesn't necessarily mean they'll earn their market value.

It's necessary to address this injustice from both ends of the spectrum. In the new fight for life, one of the pillars must be additional targeted funding for education in low-income neighborhoods. Another should be closing the wage gap that strips women of the dignity and income they deserve. Not only is this a matter of justice, but it would also be profitable for our economy.[25]

The bottom line is that if we as a nation genuinely believe in equality, our government must take drastic steps to increase funding to under-resourced schools and school districts.

One proposal developed by the Center for American Progress suggests that the government provide roughly $63 billion per year (which nets out to approximately $12,000 per student) to the 25 percent of districts with the highest poverty rate in each state.[26] Recipients would be required to use the money to improve access to education for historically underserved groups, including Black students and students from low-income families. They would also be required to set improvement targets for student outcomes, create resource equity, and report on their progress in meeting these goals.[27]

In addition, teacher training should include culturally responsive practices. "You shouldn't have some white kids who hear the Civil War was about states' rights without learning that the 'right' at issue was the power to enslave people," says Khalilah Harris, acting vice president for K–12 education policy at the Center for American Progress.[28]

There is danger in hiding certain parts of our nation's history. While power and control thrive on choosing which narratives are important, which historical figures are elevated, and what sensibilities are coddled, healing and unity come through transparency and hard, courageous conversations. A void of knowledge does not make America better or stronger.

In order to teach a more comprehensive history, new curricula will need to be adopted and new textbooks acquired. For example, there is an unprecedented K–12 curriculum that is being adopted in public schools around the country called Black History 365 (BH365). Complete with text and images, it provides an inclusive account of Black history, from ancient Africa all the way to the present day.

Current and future generations of students need a more complete understanding of our country's history—the good and the bad—in order to grasp why there is such a disparity in abortion rates, poverty, education, and employment, and to be better positioned to enact change.

Another excellent resource is the Human Dignity Curriculum (HDC). Developed by a team of researchers, anthropologists, philosophers, artists, and educators, the HDC is a K–12 curriculum that teaches students a sense of self, solidarity, and human rights. It's designed to help students better understand who they are, where they came from, and what they can become.[29] Though this is not a Christian program, it's based on the premise that all human beings have inherent dignity and value. It emphasizes virtue as a path to freedom and highlights the importance of using one's talents and abilities to serve others.[30]

"I think it's important to teach kids . . . that their dignity is a given, regardless of the situations they find themselves in, whether that's a position of illness or vulnerability or feeling small," says HDC coordinator Rocio Valdez. "Teaching young people to love themselves in the proper way and to love others without discrimination is what the HDC does."[31]

Would these educational changes be expensive to implement? Yes. But research shows that, when carefully allocated, increased funding has a significant impact on student outcomes. According to a 2015 study, increasing spending by 10 percent per student for their K–12 education resulted in wages that were 7.25 percent higher in adulthood. The effects were greatest for low-income students.[32]

Make no mistake: there will be pushback, at the federal level, at the local level, and at the personal level. This is often the case whenever an attempt is made to challenge the status quo and level the playing field between Blacks and whites. The opposition usually stems from strong feelings combined with a lack of understanding about the complexities of societal structures. Kirsten and I know people whose kids are applying to college, and when we talk to them, we often sense an undercurrent of, *If my kid doesn't get in, it's because their spot went to someone Black who's less qualified.*

When it comes to affirmative action, people tend to miss the foundational premise. Affirmative action isn't about letting less qualified people in; it's about purposefully letting in equally qualified people who historically have not been let in nearly as often—if at all.

Among flagship universities across America, my alma mater, the University of Georgia, has the second highest disparity between its proportion of Black students and Black high school graduates from the state.[33] There may be a number of factors that go into this, but it's safe to say that at least part of the problem is that doors do not open for Black students the way they do for white students.

So while it may be true that some white students won't get spots they may have gotten previously because an equally qualified Black student was given preference due to their legacy of exclusion, the data suggests that it went to another qualified white student. But that's some of the messiness that comes with trying to correct what has been wrong for so long.

As Florida professor Deandre Poole states, "When we create a society for all people and when we eradicate racism, then perhaps we could eliminate affirmative action. Until that time, we need affirmative action—and we need to strengthen it."[34] National Education Association president Becky Pringle adds, "We are stronger when our country, communities, schools, and future includes and reflects all of us. Affirmative action and programs like it safeguard a stronger future by expanding higher education opportunities to those who have been historically denied a fair shot."[35]

At this point, you may be thinking that these kinds of changes sound political or like they align with a particular party's viewpoint. But when it comes to matters of justice, it's not a partisan issue. It's a matter of finding long-term solutions that work best for individuals, communities, and society at large.

You also may be wondering what you can do, since these are systemic-level changes we're talking about. But we must have an understanding of the foundational issues underpinning abortion and recognize that to create lasting change, we can't simply treat the symptom. And we have more influence than we think, especially when we band together on these issues. I have learned that God has his people in every sector of society, from the White House to the church, from the courtroom to the living room, and he has equipped them all for every good work.

Ultimately, justice is all about restoration. In this context, it involves extending opportunities for advancement to those who have, historically, been denied them. If we are to act justly, love mercy, and walk humbly with our God (see Micah 6:8), we need to be active in our pursuit of justice.

MAKING MOTHERHOOD WORK

When my wife, Kirsten, was growing up, she dreamed of having a big corner office and going to work every day wearing a sharp business suit and heels. Then in 2000, she attended a block party at the UGA student center, where she caught the eye of an incredibly handsome, athletically gifted (and unthinkably humble) football player named Benjamin.

In 2005, we got married, and after holding off on starting a family for three years, we went full-on two-minute drill and had four kids in four and a half years. My wife was either pregnant, nursing, or both simultaneously for the better part of five years.

Two boys and two girls in, I said to Kirsten, "I think I'm done. Are you done?"

She wasn't done.

We had baby number five—a beautiful little girl named

Eden—and I said, "Okay, we've got five. Five is good. I'm good." I looked at her. "You're good, too . . . right?"

She *still* wasn't done.

After a lot of negotiation, we decided to go for number six. Why did we go for number six? Because Kirsten loves even numbers, and because when you go to Walt Disney World, everybody can hold somebody's hand—everybody has a friend.

We went for number six, and we had a miscarriage. A few months later, we tried again, and we had another miscarriage. It was devastating. We'd understood the value of life before, but when life is taken from you, it makes you truly realize the power of God described in Genesis, when it talks about how he breathed life into humankind, and how precious that life is.

I said to Kirsten, "Let's try one more time, and if there's another miscarriage, we'll be good at five."

She agreed, and a few months later, we got pregnant again.

When we went in for our twelve-week ultrasound, Kirsten, who was understandably nervous, looked at the technician. "Ma'am, do you see a baby in there? Because we've had two miscarriages."

"No . . ." she said, squinting at the screen. "I don't see one. I see *two*."

We now have seven children (and yes, she's finally done). So instead of putting on her business suit and going to a corner office every day, Kirsten has spent the past fourteen years being a mom, a part-time homeschool teacher, and CEO of our "chaordered" life. Kirsten is a great mom, and I think being a mom is one of the most important jobs there is.

As a culture, however, we've done a poor job casting motherhood. Instead of viewing it as something to be celebrated, childbearing is often framed as one of the worst things that can happen to a woman. It interferes with school, it's expensive, and it disrupts a woman's career. And all too often, the father disappears, leaving the mother to go it alone. As a result, rather than seeing pregnancy as the beginning of new life, many women perceive it as the end of the life they envisioned for themselves.

That's not to say women don't want to be mothers—many do. But they also want other things. They want to excel in their chosen field. They want to hold political positions, be professional athletes, and climb the corporate ladder. And let's face it: balancing full-time motherhood with a full-time job is no easy feat. In fact, it can feel downright impossible, which is why many women feel as though they have to choose one or the other. But what if we could create a situation where they didn't have to choose?

In this area, too, Black women are especially impacted, as they are more likely to work in low-wage, physically demanding jobs. According to Angela D. Aina, the cofounding executive director of Black Mamas Matter, "Nearly thirty percent of pregnancy discrimination complaints are filed by Black women."[36]

Dina Bakst, the cofounder and copresident of A Better Balance, says, "Black pregnant workers are disproportionately denied reasonable accommodations required to maintain a healthy pregnancy on the job." Further, those who "work in low wage and physically demanding jobs too often must risk their health at work or get pushed off the job when pregnant or after giving birth."[37]

The House of Representatives recently passed the Pregnant Workers Fairness Act, which if passed by the Senate, will minimize the risk pregnant women face at work and grant them more economic security.[38] Legislation aside, all employers should be willing to make allowances for women during those critical months when new life is maturing inside their womb.

These considerations don't have to be monumental. Sometimes it's as simple as providing a stool for a woman to sit on so she doesn't have to stand on an assembly line for eight hours a day. It might mean having a designated quiet room where she can lie down for a few moments if needed. Or it may involve lightened duties during the final trimester to avoid unnecessary strain—especially in physically demanding jobs. Policies like these could make a world of difference not only for the health of the child but in a woman's decision to carry her baby to term. They cost little yet send an invaluable message to the employee that the organization values her and wants to keep her there.

Beyond those nine months, the first twelve weeks of a newborn's life are critical for both the baby and the mother. It's a time to bond, recover, and adjust to a new rhythm of life. I vividly remember the excitement of the first twelve weeks of our children's lives. I also remember how exhausted we were and how hard it was for Kirsten to be mom to our other children while recovering from delivery and caring for a newborn.

At present, paid maternity leave is not mandated by the federal government, and Medicaid provides benefits for only the first sixty days postpartum, which is not nearly enough. And while the Family and Medical Leave Act guarantees twelve weeks of unpaid, job-protected leave following the birth of a newborn or the adoption of a child, not everyone qualifies for it (and not everyone can afford to take it). In fact, it is estimated that only 21 percent of the American workforce has access to paid maternity leave.[39] Not surprisingly, those with lower-paying service jobs have far less access to paid leave.

What this means is that companies implement their own maternity leave policies at their discretion. As a result, some women receive several months of paid leave, while others don't have any. These women are forced to return to work prematurely or risk losing their jobs.

There is some good news, however. COVID-19 has presented an unprecedented opportunity for changes in maternity policies. The pandemic resulted in upward of three million women leaving the workforce, and corporations are "waking up to the economic benefits of larger-scale social support for families."[40] But much like the education debt, a strong bipartisan effort will be required to right this wrong. While such legislation isn't directly related to abortion, a sharp increase in paid maternity leave would send a positive pro-life message to mothers and employers alike.

The pandemic also resulted in a greater acceptance of remote work in some companies. If a woman has a new baby or a child who isn't in school yet, being able to work from home several days a week gives her more time with her children and lessens the financial burden of childcare.

With more people working from home, many companies now have a surplus of office space. Why not convert some of that space into on-site childcare? While there would undoubtedly be start-up expenses, the benefits of keeping good, experienced workers and the reduction in absenteeism would likely save companies money in the long run. "Forward-thinking employers [know] that, if they [can] help working mothers . . . come to work, and help relieve some of that burden, and the mental load of taking care of children, they will have more productive employees," says Maribeth Bearfield, chief human resources officer at Bright Horizons, the country's largest provider of employer-sponsored childcare.[41]

Kirsten interned for Chick-fil-A at their corporate office the summer before her senior year in college. We weren't married yet, and kids were nowhere on the radar, but she still appreciated the on-site day care that was provided for employees, which allowed mothers (and fathers) to remain close to their children while at work. Mothers could even take time to nurse throughout the day if necessary. The point is that efforts like this build a culture of life and show an appreciation for motherhood and parenting.

There are a variety of ways companies can support working moms. Former news correspondent for ABC News and working mom Paula Faris cites several in her book *You Don't Have to Carry It All: Ditch the Mom Guilt and Find a Better Way Forward.* Here are a few ideas: "providing childcare stipends, designating 'moms only' spaces for moms who need to nurse or pump during the work day, establishing programs to onboard moms returning to work, encouraging self-care by offering paid time off for 'mental health' days, and establishing sponsorship programs geared at training and equipping mothers to lead, and actually hiring women in key leadership positions."[42]

It's all about changing the narrative that having a baby will ruin a woman's life. So when a woman facing an unplanned pregnancy says, "I'm not able to raise a child because I'll lose my job" or "I can't afford day care on my salary," we can say, "Have you considered asking your employer about working remotely a few days a week or helping you cover the cost of childcare?" Of course, this isn't an option for everyone, and working from home comes with its own set of challenges. But it may be part of a larger conversation about things that need to change for women in the workplace.

"One of the things that the pandemic has done is [push employers to start] seeing workers as human beings that have needs, instead of as commodities that can be swapped out and easily replaced," says economist Diane Swonk. "That's a major shift and it is giving workers a moment of bargaining power they have not had, particularly for women who have already gotten the short end of the stick."[43]

"Whoever thought your employer would pay your babysitter for you, but employers are starting to do that," says Bearfield.[44] Sometimes the difference between choosing life or death is simply a matter of challenging people out of their current narratives and helping them envision possibilities they didn't even know were there.

Which leads me to my final suggestion . . .

WE NEED A BETTER PLAN FOR PARENTHOOD

In 2021, Planned Parenthood, which accounts for about 40 percent of abortions in the US, received $633 million in government funding. Right now, they are sitting on $2.1 billion in net assets.[45] They are, quite frankly, a behemoth. And even though privately funded pregnancy resource centers outnumber Planned Parenthood clinics fourteen to one,[46] all their marketing budgets combined would amount to only a fraction of Planned Parenthood's marketing budget.

Planned Parenthood's advertising is everywhere— schools, hospitals, college campuses, billboards, magazines, doctors' offices, television, and online. They even launched a $16 million ad campaign in advance of the Supreme Court reversal in 2022 to make women dealing with unplanned pregnancies nationwide aware of their services and locations.[47]

Planned Parenthood strives to be the first organization women think about when they find themselves with an unwanted pregnancy and the easiest phone number to find when they're on the fence about a preborn child. And though Planned Parenthood does offer other services such as STD testing and treatment, cancer screenings, birth control, and some primary care, abortion is far and away their greatest revenue source. In fact, Planned Parenthood performs forty-three abortions for every prenatal care service they provide.[48] On their website, they actively discourage women from visiting privately run, faith-based pregnancy resource centers, making false claims about those organizations' motives:

Other family planning centers, private doctors, and abortion providers may also talk with you about your decision. But when you're looking for a reliable health center, beware of anti-abortion "crisis pregnancy centers." These are places that may seem like normal medical clinics and claim to offer information about pregnancy options and abortion, but they don't provide abortion or a full range of health care. They often give you false or misleading information about pregnancy, abortion, and birth control. . . . Crisis pregnancy centers are often located very close to Planned Parenthood health centers or other real medical centers, and have similar names—they do this to confuse people and trick them into visiting them instead.[49]

Choosing to bring new life into this world is not a business decision, nor should a frightened and vulnerable young woman be viewed as a customer. She needs compassion and tenderness, not a sales pitch designed to push her into making a rash decision.

I recently spoke at a banquet in Chicago as part of a fundraiser for a network of pregnancy resource centers. As part of the program, several young women with unplanned pregnancies shared their stories, as did the PRC counselors who came alongside them.

One of these stories in particular stood out to me. Her name is Lisa, and she became pregnant in her early twenties. "My mom worked twelve- to sixteen-hour shifts . . . to put food on the table and for us to have a roof over our heads," she shares. "When I found out that I was pregnant, I knew my mom wasn't going to take it lightly. . . . But at the end of the day, that's my mom, and I knew she was going to find out eventually . . . so I told her. And she said, 'I would like for you to think about getting an abortion.'"[50]

Unsure of what to do, she reached out to her local pregnancy resource center, where she met Heather.

"She wanted to parent, but she just didn't have the support or the tools or the resources to be able to do it," Heather explains. "All the outside influences in her life . . . were really wearing her down and really pressuring her, and she just needed somebody to hold her and hug her and validate her and tell her that she's amazing and strong and capable—just being that rock of support for her, because when she walks out those doors, she has no other source of support. She has no one on her team. She has no one, no one to uplift her."

A few days later, Lisa came in to get an ultrasound. "My mom came with me, because I thought it would be a great idea if she heard his heartbeat as well," she says. They got even more than a heartbeat. "He was, like, waving," she recalls, smiling. "And it was so cute, and then my mom just fell in love."

Lisa continues, "When I walked out of there . . . Heather asked if she could keep in touch with me during the pregnancy and after. So she was very supportive throughout. . . . Whatever I needed help with, they would provide it for me . . . counseling, therapy, housing . . . I didn't have to hesitate to ask. They would just provide me with all of that."

Heather explains, "It's not just like we just leave them, like 'You chose life . . . okay, great.' We really want to walk them through that experience, because those obstacles are still there, those stresses are still there, that pain is still there. It was just a great gift to be able to be there for her for those nine months, to speak those words of truth . . . to be that source of love and support and encouragement, and to just say, 'You can do this. You've got this.'"

Imagine if the government redirected some of its funding to PRCs so more women could get the kind of caring, long-term support Lisa received.

At present, PRCs are recipients of some government money, block grants, and state funds, but 90 percent of their funding is from private and local sources. And 80 percent of centers receive no government funding at all.[51] In this new post-*Roe* world, every state needs to support pregnancy resource centers—especially those in "abortion haven" states like Illinois, Colorado, and New York, where the need is the greatest.

Likewise, federally qualified health centers (FQHCs) provide comprehensive health care—including prenatal care—for tens of millions of low-income men, women, and children. Typically located in rural communities, these centers service counties with no obstetric hospitals or birth centers and no obstetric providers. Given that 36 percent of counties across the US are currently designated as maternity-care deserts, government funding for these centers is vital.[52]

Yet the pro-choice industry and its government allies seem committed to attacking the type of life-affirming free assistance offered at PRCs and FQHCs, opting instead to throw their support behind Planned Parenthood and other like-minded organizations, to the point of lobbying for the establishment of abortion facilities rather than maternity-care centers on federal land.[53]

"Women deserve life-affirming solutions to critical healthcare shortages," says Live Action researcher Carole Novielli. "What they don't need are unregulated virtual and mobile abortion options, and chemical abortion pills. It is past time for policymakers to pivot from abortion advocacy to building real healthcare options for women."[54]

Finally, our country's foster-care system is in need of additional funding, at both the state level and the national level. There are currently more than 400,000 children living in foster care in the US,[55] and 48 percent of the girls in foster care become pregnant by age nineteen.[56] The foster care system would benefit from having more social workers and from working in conjunction with faith-based foster programs to recruit and support more foster parents. Improving the child-welfare system will not only help children find the loving homes they deserve but also help prevent unplanned pregnancies.

THE COST OF JUSTICE

Earlier in this chapter, I shared the quote from Dr. Martin Luther King Jr. about how we tend to be "uneasy with injustice but unwilling yet to pay a significant price to eradicate it."

None of the proposed solutions outlined in this chapter are simple, quick, or cheap. Problems that have been compounding over hundreds of years don't resolve overnight. Most require federal funding, which of course equates to tax dollars. Whether this federal support comes in the form of guaranteed cash payments, increased child tax credits, scholarships, stipends to offset the cost of childcare, support for failing schools, support for PRCs, or improvements to the foster care system, one thing is certain: going on the offense to make broken people whole is a higher calling than simply defending them from discrimination. A pro-life commitment to justice recognizes the causal links between past and present injustices and is willing to act.

Louisiana state senator Katrina Jackson once told me, "The next level of advocacy is making sure that we're passing state and federal laws that enable people to have a piece of the American dream."[57] I believe she's right. And I believe the time is now.

It's going to take intentionality. It's going to take resources. And it's going to take sacrifices—from all of us.

After all, no one ever said life—or the fight for it—would be easy.

CHAPTER 7

THE BODY OF CHRIST

We don't want condemnation. We want grace. We want also for people
to understand if they get themselves in a situation where they have
an unplanned pregnancy, they shouldn't have to run from the church;
they should be running to it.

CHERILYN HOLLOWAY

According to a study by the National Campaign to Prevent Teen and Unplanned Pregnancy, 80 percent of evangelicals between the ages of eighteen and twenty-nine have had premarital sex.[1] Further statistics show that roughly 40 percent of babies in the United States are born outside of marriage.[2]

In her book *Sex, Jesus, and the Conversations Church Forgot,* Mo Isom contends, "If we deeply understood the physical, mental, emotional, and above all, spiritual definition of and implications of sex, I don't think these numbers would look anywhere near the same. I don't think they could."[3]

I agree wholeheartedly. However, it's hard for people to understand a topic that is rarely—if ever—discussed. That's why I believe it's vital that we start having more authentic,

God-honoring conversations about sex—both at home and in the church.

AN OUNCE OF PREVENTION

Obviously, the easiest way to make abortion unthinkable and unnecessary is to eliminate unplanned pregnancies in the first place. That ends primarily with teens and adults making responsible decisions, but it starts with talking openly, honestly, and lovingly with our children about sex.

As a father, I understand that talking to your children about sex can be awkward. But if we don't talk to them, they'll learn about it through the media's distorted lens, from the Internet, or from friends who know even less than they do.

I know from experience how hilarious these conversations can be. Once, after two of my younger kids saw Kirsten and me kiss twice in a row, their eyes got wide with excitement. They pointed at us and squealed, "You did it twice! Now you're gonna have twins again!" The older kids, of course, said, "Yeah . . . that's not how it works."

Another time, my son asked me where he was before he was born. When I pointed to the designated area of my body, the look on his face was priceless. Needless to say, we had a long conversation after that. As awkward as I felt, however, I knew how important it was to have this conversation with my son. I just had to get over my own embarrassment.

Frankly, it's worth it to be uncomfortable for a few minutes every now and then if it means our kids grow up with a healthy understanding of sex. At some point, maybe even in the near future, they'll run into somebody at school or on a sports team who has gotten pregnant and is considering an abortion—and it might even be them.

Case in point: my daughter is in seventh grade, and the other day, she got to school a little bit early. She went to the lunchroom where everybody hangs out until it's time to go to class. She happened to walk in on a conversation a handful of girls were having. One said, "I don't ever want to have kids." Another girl casually replied, "Well, if you did get pregnant, you could always just abort it."

And this is seventh grade.

At a Christian school.

That's why it's imperative that we talk to our daughters and sons about God's design for sex early and often. The family was the first institution God established. Within the walls of our homes, we are charged with loving our spouses and raising our kids in the admonition of the Lord. There is no greater influence over a child's life than that of a parent. That means there should be no topic we shy away from with our children. That includes sexuality.

The problem is that each of us carries some sort of sexual baggage into our relationships. That hurt, guilt, shame, or fear can be an obstacle to speaking the loving truth our children desperately need to hear. Whether or not we grew up with parents that normalized these conversations, we must realize how our willingness to engage transparently will determine the trajectory of our children's lives, possibly saving them from future heartache and disappointment.

I remember having those conversations with my father. They weren't frequent, but they were straightforward, especially when I was a teenager. "Your body was made with systems that respond to certain stimuli. Don't start something you can't and shouldn't be finishing."

I was talking to a friend of mine, and he said that when he was thirteen, his grandfather gave him a handful of condoms, telling him, "Here, make sure you use these." That was it. What kind of message is that? Unfortunately, it was probably the same message a trusted man in his own life had given him.

My boys are still young. But as they grow older, I plan to keep the conversation going, with even more frequency and honesty than I experienced as a child. Each generation has the opportunity to build on what was and was not taught to them in the home. But one thing I learned from my father that I will be sure to pass on to my sons is the four *p*'s.

PRIEST, PROPHET, PROTECTOR, AND PROVIDER

Paul gave this command to the Corinthian church, and while it applies to all believers, I think the message is especially important for men to hear and internalize: "Be on guard. Stand firm in the faith. Be courageous. Be strong" (1 Corinthians 16:13). To that end, my daddy always said men need to be the priest, prophet, protector, and provider for their home.

In biblical times, the priest offered sacrifices for the forgiveness of the people. Now obviously I'm not suggesting we go to the backyard and kill a sheep, but Daddy impressed on me early and often that as a man, I need to pray for my family and go before the Lord for them—not just for the big test they have coming up in school or for healing when they're not feeling well, but for their spiritual struggles as well.

As prophets, men need to intentionally set aside time to read the Word of God and expound on it to their families. I vividly remember my father reading the book of Genesis to my siblings and me as a child, and now I do the same thing with my kids. It's nothing super formal. We just read a chapter every couple of nights, and then we reflect on what it's about (chapter 1, the Creation story; chapter 2, the creation of man and woman; chapter 3, the fall of humankind; chapter 4, Cain and Abel, and so on). I love the book of Genesis because it's about foundations, and it's important to give our kids a biblical framework for seeing the world. In a world where trends are seen as truth, God's truths never change.

When it comes to being protectors, men are usually pretty good in terms of physical protection. I mean, most men would happily take a bullet for their kids. But we also need to protect their hearts by putting guardrails around the things they do, the places they go, and the people they associate with, so they won't be led astray or fall victim to peer pressure.

Kirsten and I are especially cautious when it comes to social media and the Internet. Scripture warns us not to look at anything vulgar (see Psalm 101:3) and not to "copy the behavior and customs of this world" (Romans 12:2). At some point, our kids will stumble across something online they shouldn't see. That's why we need to be preemptive, keep the lines of communication open, and make sure our kids feel safe coming to us with questions.

Right around the time I started college, my daddy told me, "Son, if you don't have a job and you still need help taking care of yourself, you are not ready to take on anybody else. Now, that doesn't mean you have to be able to provide a mansion, but if you want to be a daddy and a husband, you'd better be able to provide something."

Given that upward of 200,000 children go into the child-welfare system every year,[4] I'd say Daddy's advice was pretty spot on. More often than not, when we're talking about the decision to choose life, the fatherhood piece makes all the difference.

THE DIFFERENCE A DAD MAKES

In the previous chapter, we talked about the importance of elevating and honoring motherhood. But children need a positive male influence in their lives too. Children who grow up without a father are four times more likely to grow up in poverty and twice as likely to drop out of school. They are more likely to abuse drugs and alcohol, and more likely to go to prison. Girls who grow up without fathers are seven times more likely to become pregnant as teens.[5] Further, abortion-determined women list the lack of support from the baby's father as one of the primary obstacles to choosing life. With all this in mind, I can't overstate the importance of men's role in the new fight for life.

Fatherhood begins with the man's relationship with the baby's mother before the baby arrives. How does he treat her? How does he love her and care for her? How does he respect her, talk about her, and support her? Most men learn how to treat a woman by example, and unfortunately, whether due to neglect or extenuating circumstances, too many children grow up without a father figure in the house to emulate.

THE BODY OF CHRIST || 165

Society at large has a tendency to present fathers in a negative light. There's a pervasive narrative that fathers are uninvolved, thus normalizing the absentee dad. When you look at TV shows, the dad is typically depicted as a goofy, clueless dude who is of little assistance to his wife and has no idea what's going on with his kids.

Many of my conversations with young men involve telling them that their role *is* important and that whether or not they had a dad growing up, they still have what it takes. In fact, a lot of the guys I talk to are worried about replicating the bad behavior they saw from their own fathers. On the flip side, there are a lot of guys who tell me, "I can't wait to be a dad because I'm going to do everything my dad did *not* do."

I've been a dad for more than a decade now, and I can promise you I've made my fair share of mistakes. But the stats don't lie: even an imperfect dad is better than no dad at all. We are all flawed, yet we must strive to be present. The post-*Roe* world needs strong, courageous, compassionate dads. Mothers need them. Children need them. Society needs them. And the church needs them.

I firmly believe that abortion will end when men make it so. That's not to say that women don't have a role to play. What I'm saying is that if we men did what we're supposed to do on a family level, a parenting level, a government level, a mission level, a church level, and a philanthropic level— defend the voiceless—we wouldn't be wrestling with all these social crises.

The enemy would tell men that they don't have what it takes. But the truth is, when men are submitted to God and committed to their families, they will train up arrows that pierce the culture (see Psalm 127:4), bringing about a harvest of change and shining liberating light where there was once a cloak of darkness.

As Christian men, we must understand the power we possess to speak life into the hearts of our families and commit to being emotionally, physically, and spiritually involved in the lives of our children.

WHAT ARE WE AFRAID OF?

In many respects, I believe the new fight for life is a spiritual battle. A big part of Satan's plan to destroy humankind is to go after men's relationships with women. That's exactly what he did in the Garden: he pitted Adam against Eve, and after he turned them against each other, he went after their children.

From the very beginning, Satan has perverted sex, using it to ruin relationships instead of enhancing them, exploiting people instead of uplifting them, and destroying life instead of creating it. And he's still doing this today.

Sex has a hold on us unlike anything else. That's why it's one of his most frequently used weapons. As mother of four Mo Isom writes,

> Our culture is saturated with [sex]. . . . Our
> televisions ooze it. . . . Magazines and books and
> apps and social media outlets stream it down
> our throats. . . . We're obsessed with it. . . . We're
> entertained by it. . . . While society twists, perverts,
> cheapens, and idolizes it, we—the church—are

relatively silent about it. Awkwardly stumbling around it. Running from it. Building desperate rule lists of do's and don'ts. . . . Somewhere along the way we've allowed ourselves to be drowned out of the conversation. . . . [But] it's our responsibility to talk about it. . . . It is a topic fiercely close to God's heart, a topic that flows from the pages of His Word. . . . God, after all, is the inventor of sex. We were made, by Him, as sexual beings. So if it's a topic fiercely close to His heart, it must become a topic fiercely close to ours. . . . Reclaiming sex as the act of holy worship God always intended it to be isn't taboo or embarrassing—it's eternity-shifting. . . . It's time to begin reclaiming sex for the glory of God. . . . It's time to start the conversations that the church forgot.[6]

Once again, Mo is spot on. Churches don't talk about sex nearly enough, which is ironic, given that the first command God gives man and woman is to "be fruitful and multiply" (Genesis 1:28). I mean, sex is sitting right there—before God talks about how we should live or how we should tithe. Before any other rules, laws, or commandments are issued, God institutes sex.

We see the full spectrum of sexual relationships in the Bible: marital sex, adultery, incest, homosexuality, even rape. Money aside, sex is part of more biblical narratives than virtually any other topic. In fact, other than the Holy Spirit, sex might be the single most powerful force described in Scripture.

That's why we need to start talking about it more—from the pulpit, in Sunday school, and in small groups. According to author and youth leader Scott Gillenwaters, "One of the best things about churches teaching sexuality is we can get away with teaching a broader curriculum than schools or other places. We can teach the biology of the human body, contraception and sexually transmitted diseases (STDs), but we can also share our views on sexual morality and conduct." Gillenwaters continues, "A school may get into trouble if a health teacher speaks for or against abortion, but the church can be very honest about that topic. A school can't say intercourse outside of marriage is a sin because that crosses a line schools don't like to cross. Churches, however, can share their views on the subject without public recourse."[7]

I recently worked with an organization called Stand for Life on the development of a six-week curriculum designed for use in churches. It's intended to help both children and adults gain a solid biblical foundation on human dignity and what it means to be created in the image of God, specifically as it relates to the pro-life discussion and our responsibility as believers.

The resources are there. We just have to get past the social stigma and our own embarrassment over talking about sex in a church setting and engage in the conversation.

TEACH THEM WELL

Research shows that kids start forming ideas about sex as early as five years old, and by the time they're ten, many are already beginning to experiment both on their own and with friends.[8] In addition to teaching our children how God provided for Noah, how he parted the Red Sea, and how he helped David conquer Goliath, Sunday school curricula need to talk about how Delilah used her sexuality to trick Samson, how David lusted after Bathsheba, and how Jesus redeemed the woman at the well and the woman caught in the act of adultery.[9] Kids need to understand what adultery is, why God calls it a sin, and how God designed sexual intimacy to strengthen and celebrate the marital union between a man and a woman.

And while the church should definitely teach the importance of sexual purity, it's not enough to just say, "It's a sin to have sex before marriage, so don't do it." As the father of seven, I can promise you that nothing makes a willful, curious child want to try something more than an adult telling them no. If we simply issue an ultimatum, we miss the opportunity to talk about *why* it's better to wait. And the *why* is where the real learning happens.

God designed sex to be an expression of physical, emotional, and spiritual love and connection between a husband and a wife. He designed it for our pleasure, and within the covenant of marriage, it is to be enjoyed to the fullest. If we limit our discussion solely to the mechanics, kids may wrongly believe sex is only a physical act. They need to be taught that healthy sexuality between a husband and a wife requires emotional and spiritual intimacy as well.[10]

And while the church needs to be a place where we don't compromise on sexual purity or God's design for sex, it must also be a place where young people can feel safe coming for counsel if and when they fall short of these standards. They already feel bad enough—they don't need to be humiliated and told how terrible they are. They need someone to help them.

Unfortunately, many churches and believers default to legalism, like the ancient Pharisees who criticized Jesus for healing on the Sabbath. The problem with this shame-based approach is that there's no space for grace or forgiveness. When a brother or sister is condemned for falling short, the guilt they feel may keep them from setting foot in a church or spending time with its people again. When an unplanned pregnancy hits, where will they turn?

Sin always has both individual and corporate consequences. But where sin abounds, grace abounds much more.

KEEPING UP APPEARANCES

There's an old saying that the church is the only army that shoots its own wounded. When it comes to the church's treatment of unwed mothers, that saying often holds true.

New life should always be a cause for celebration. But when that new life doesn't come with a wedding band attached, we get uncomfortable and judgmental—especially in the church.

Granted, churches should hold their members to a higher standard. And why not? Paul tells us that we are to "live in such a way that no one will stumble because of us, and no one will find fault with our ministry" (2 Corinthians 6:3). It should be saddening when a professed believer has a baby out of wedlock or impregnates someone out of wedlock. But that doesn't mean we shouldn't care for that person and their circumstances. After all, "we all fall short of God's glorious standard" (Romans 3:23).

Yet all too often we respond to spiritual missteps by shooting our own—casting out sinners, lest we, too, be seen as guilty by association. The more visible the sin, the bigger the target we place on the offender's back. Undoubtedly, the church is called to lovingly yet unequivocally address unrepentant sin, especially among those in leadership. If it fails to do so, it's merely a country club without the golf cart and eighteen holes. But the church also needs to be a place for the sick to be healed and restored.

In 1 Corinthians 6, Paul instructs the church about dealing with lawsuits among believers. In verses 9-10 he lists a litany of sins, such as dishonesty, drunkenness, idolatry, greed, sex outside of marriage, adultery, and homosexuality. He concludes, "Some of you used to be like this. But you were washed, you were sanctified, you were justified in the name of the Lord Jesus Christ and by the Spirit of God" (see verse 11). Lest these believers forget their own redeemed wretchedness, Paul sends them a timely reminder. It is foolish and prideful to forget where we were yesterday, but we also need to remember how the Spirit of God has transformed us today. For many of us, that transformation occurs in the fellowship of the saints.

We should be mindful of how harshly we treat those who have committed visible sins or sins that haven't befallen us personally. Sins such as drunkenness and greed may be easier to hide than a same-sex relationship or a pregnant belly from an extramarital relationship, but all these sins need to be cleansed by the blood.

As Christians, we want to look like we have everything under control. We want to look like we're obedient. That's why we're more concerned with the sin that gets found out than the sin that doesn't.

A similar phenomenon happens in football. There's an altercation of some kind at the end of a play, and someone mumbles something under their breath. Tempers flare, and the next thing you know, a fight breaks out. Here's the thing, though—the guy who started the fight rarely gets called for the penalty. That's because the refs don't usually see the first punch. They do, however, see the other guy hitting back. Both are guilty, but the refs only penalize the guy who gets caught.

All too often, instead of rallying around unwed mothers with the love and support they desperately need, we blink back the logs in our own eyes and push these women away. But abortion will never become unthinkable until the church stops exercising its own hypocrisy: professing to value all human life, yet only embracing life that has been conceived within the bounds of matrimony.

In his book *Dangerous Jesus*, Christian hip-hop artist KB writes,

> We all agree that a baby is a gift from God, and therefore we want single mothers to safely bring their babies into this world out of their duty to God. Yet our actions often don't communicate that those babies born out of wedlock are as valuable to God as those born in wedlock. We don't celebrate them as we should. We don't congratulate the unwed mother

on bringing new life into the world. If we genuinely
cherished new life, we would rally around the unwed
mother, love her, and help her take care of the new
life that we claim to value and fight to protect.

The salient reality is that we often don't know
how to say that sex outside of marriage is a sin
while at the same time honoring what that sex
might produce. New life is to be praised, protected,
and provided for—and that includes our *active*
participation. But too often we prioritize the
rhetoric of premarital abstinence over the reality
of loving and caring for our unwed neighbors.
Legislation is but a single way to protect life in the
womb. . . . But grace-driven love for both women
and their babies, regardless of the context, creates a
culture of life that abortion cannot survive.[11]

I know a woman in Nashville who hosted a church fellowship group at her house every Sunday night. One evening,
a young woman showed up at her door unannounced and
said, "I'd like to join your small group, but I think you should
know, I'm pregnant and I'm not married. If you're not comfortable with that, I understand." Having come from a legal-
istic background, she was worried that she might not be well
received by members of her conservative Christian church.

But the group welcomed her with open arms. Over the
course of the next several months, they helped her set up a
nursery and bought diapers, formula, baby clothes, and other
supplies. They threw her a baby shower, and after her little
girl was born, they took turns babysitting and having mother

and baby over for dinner. The little girl is now four years old, and her extended church family still throws her birthday parties and helps the mother out whenever they can.

"She wasn't destitute," my friend said. "She had a college degree and a job. She was just lonely and frightened and struggling. People don't realize how challenging it is to raise a child by yourself. More than anything, she needed emotional, relational, and spiritual support." Fortunately, this woman fell into a nest of nurturing Southern women who gave her the practical help and encouragement she needed.

"We've been taking care of her and her little girl for almost five years now. We've listened to her, held her while she cried, counseled her, and prayed for and over her. We didn't pursue her—she just showed up at our door. To drive to a stranger's house, knock on the door, and say, 'I'd like to join your group, but I think you should know . . .' was incredibly brave. Of course we were going to help her."

THE IMPORTANCE OF COMMUNITY

In some ways, my career has trained me to be a loner. For the better part of two decades, my family lived in a place for two or three years, maybe four, and then I'd sign with a new team. We'd pack up the kids and move to the next place. By the time we'd get locked into a church, it was time to leave again. And because we knew we'd be uprooted at some point, we didn't exercise the muscle of connecting. Instead, we kept people at a measured distance, if for no other reason than to save ourselves from the emotional pain of making new friends only to leave them behind. We know firsthand that not having a close church community can be incredibly isolating.

When Kirsten and I suffered our two miscarriages, we had just relocated to Baltimore and hadn't plugged into a church yet. We didn't know anybody in our neighborhood, and we didn't have family nearby, so we didn't have much spiritual support. As a result, we suffered in silence, and it was miserable. Now that I'm retired and we've begun to put down roots, we're starting to get more involved in our church community. But we haven't forgotten what that isolation was like.

Too many Christians, I believe, have a consumer mentality. We come to church on Sundays to get fed and be encouraged, but we don't put anything back in. We don't exercise our gifts to build up the body, and we don't experience real community. Without community, there's no support. And make no mistake: the new fight for life will require us to band together.

American sociologist Rodney Stark writes, "Christianity did not grow because of miracle working in the marketplaces (although there may have been much of that going on), or because Constantine said it should, or even because the martyrs gave it such credibility. It grew because Christians constituted an intense community."[12] This community resulted in "a miniature welfare state in an empire which for the most part lacked social services."[13]

Historically, the church has served as the moral conscience of society. The early Christians treated strangers as neighbors and neighbors as family. They showed compassionate care for the poor. When plagues hit, they remained in the city to take care of the sick. When the Romans abandoned unwanted newborns in the fields to be eaten by wild animals or to die in the elements, Christians would take them in and raise them as their own.[14]

That's what being a community of believers looks like. What makes the church a distinctive force in society is not our separation from it but our willingness to actively engage with it.

Russell Moore, a public theologian who serves as editor in chief for *Christianity Today*, writes, "A church that loses its distinctiveness is a church that has nothing distinctive with which to engage the culture. A worldly church is of no good to the world."[15] He goes on to explain that "if we simply dissolve into the culture around us, or refuse to leave untroubled the questions the culture deems too sensitive to ask, we are not on mission at all."[16] Ultimately, "a Christianity that is walled off from the culture around it is a Christianity that dies."[17] Amen to that.

THE POWER OF THE BLACK CHURCH

On a warm October day in 2018, Kirsten and I made a twenty-minute trip across town for a meeting at the Andrew P. Sanchez community center in the Lower Ninth Ward in New Orleans. Upon arriving, we checked in at the front desk, and because I avoid taking the stairs at all costs during the football season, we took the elevator to the second floor. There, one of four local Baptist Community Health Services centers offered affordable comprehensive medical and behavioral health care to neighborhood residents, including ultrasounds using a machine we'd recently donated and were dedicating that day.

When we got off the elevator, we were met by a familiar face. I hadn't seen Pastor Fred Luter Jr. since he spoke at a pregame chapel years before. A New Orleans native, Pastor Luter was raised in the same area the community center was located. In 1986, he took the reins of Franklin Avenue Baptist Church. Once an all-white congregation, the church became mostly Black after white families moved out of the neighborhood in the 1970s and 1980s. He has always had a deep love for the church and a passion for speaking out in defense of life for the preborn child.

By 2005, the church had grown from a few hundred members to more than seven thousand. Then the storm came. In the aftermath of Hurricane Katrina, the church was buried under eight feet of water, scattering the flock to cities all over Louisiana and beyond. Being the good shepherd he is, Pastor Luter traveled the country, preaching and caring for distraught members in Houston, Baton Rouge, and Atlanta.

I'll never forget the carnage Kirsten and I witnessed as we drove through the Lower Ninth in the spring of 2006. Unsalvageable furniture, flood-soaked mattresses, and inoperable vehicles still littered the narrow streets. We stopped in astonishment, imagining the horrors the residents must have endured. We witnessed the ominous X codes, which have since found their way into New Orleans art and culture. These spray-painted markings told the stories of life, death, and destruction in each dwelling. Though final death toll estimates were inconclusive, the victims were often Black and skewed older.[18]

Nearly two decades later, the neighborhood looks much different. Franklin Avenue Baptist Church has recovered and been rebuilt, although many displaced New Orleanians never returned. Pastor Luter is still leading the flock, and he is still an outspoken advocate for life. In a recent interview, he lamented, "Not a lot of African Americans are speaking out about [abortion] . . . and a lot of preachers don't talk about it from the pulpit."[19]

Unfortunately, he's correct. The church has been silent for too long on an issue that impacts four in ten women (and men) sitting in our pews.[20]

The response to the *Dobbs* decision was mixed in Black churches. While some church leaders were elated by the news, others were less enthusiastic. Several well-known Black pastors even condemned what they considered an egregious attack on women's rights, doubling down on a pro-choice agenda from the pulpit. In speaking with one of these pastors, I was told that this isn't necessarily because they fully support abortion. He claimed that it's because they don't align ideologically with pro-life politicians and because the socioeconomic challenges their congregations face make abortion access a necessary if undesirable option. Candidly, many Black believers and congregations, even those staunchly against abortion, struggle to use the term *pro-life* because it is so intertwined with a Republican party they don't identify with. As a result, the reversal of *Roe* has been met with a complex reception rather than the sheer jubilation exhibited by many white evangelical circles.

My desire here is not to manufacture conflict or highlight a split between Black people of faith. I hope not to set people against one another or to abet a majority culture that platforms a safe, agreeable Black person as an example for the others to follow. Too many forces over the last four hundred years have tried to destroy unity among the Black community for me to create strife over unnecessary critique. But when abortion has been given unfettered reign to silently kill our most precious gifts, I find it appalling to witness such feeble responses from those in spiritual leadership. Politics is one thing; preaching is another. Some of our most well-known shepherds are leading their flock over a cliff for a bag of silver and a fleeting moment of popularity. Instead of calling out the value of life amid every attack on human dignity, including policing, incarceration, poverty, elder care, voting rights, and abortion, some leaders have drawn a line of distinction when it comes to the rights of preborn children.

As someone who values both life and justice, I don't think the two are mutually exclusive. I believe the church should be a prophetic voice in the culture—preaching God's Word, standing on principle, being the conscience of the nation—while at the same time influencing politics and cultural trends.

For many Black folks in America, the church has long been a cornerstone. Though times have changed, it is still an anchor and a respected (if not revered) institution. That said, the Black church is not a monolith. Like all institutions, it has changed from generation to generation, and the role it plays in the community is as varied as the melanin in our skin. But although each church family is different, the Black church in general is often credited with having a strong sense of justice, an adherence to biblical inerrancy, and a distinct cultural tradition.

Because of their history of enduring and overcoming as a people, Black faith communities have been free from the dualism that often encumbers white believers at the crossroads of Jesus and justice. The Black church has always believed it's possible—in fact, necessary—to take a stand on social issues while also following Jesus. From people like Sojourner Truth to Dr. King to Pastor Luter, the Black church has woven a biblical understanding of justice into the fabric of their faith.

As I've talked to white brothers and sisters in Christ over the last several years, I've discovered that some are highly orthodox when it comes to doctrine and the tenets of the faith but consider racial equality and acts of service as an elective. Others, meanwhile, are prepared to march for every cause of justice but are unfamiliar with the biblical doctrine that drives it. The gospel itself—the deity, death, burial, and resurrection of Jesus—is of utmost importance when it comes to saving souls, but we demonstrate its power and our love for our neighbor in the way we live it out.

As church history professor Vince Bantu explains, the Black church tradition "is concerned with both orthodoxy and orthopraxy"—that is, right belief and right conduct. "The Black church, wrought with unimaginable oppression and undergirded by the power of the Gospel of Jesus Christ, has always understood the inseparable nature of biblical truth and justice," says Bantu. "The same Gospel that empowered African-American Christians to fight for freedom from slavery is now crying out for justice from a racist and unjust policing and incarceration system that disproportionately penalizes people of color for financial profit in ways very similar to slavery and Jim Crow segregation."[21]

When you consider the economic, vocational, and educational obstacles that lead to abortion, it's clear that the

Black church is uniquely positioned to be a prophetic voice of influence. The gospel compels us all to be beacons of light and liberators for the oppressed, and with the history of oppression in the US, the Black church can speak into these topics in a powerful way.

As a child growing up in predominantly Black churches, I distinctly recall being engulfed by a love for the Lord and believing he desired both the salvation of souls and the liberation of bodies. History reveals that Black clergy have often led this charge, fighting for justice for their communities. In 1865, Baptist minister Garrison Frazier, along with nineteen other ministers, met with Union general William Sherman and Secretary of War Edwin Stanton to advocate for land for formerly enslaved men, women, and children. A few days later, President Lincoln approved, and Sherman issued Special Field Orders No. 15, commonly referred to as "forty acres and a mule."[22]

When the Methodist church in colonial America treated its Black congregants poorly, dragging praying Blacks away from the front of the church, ministers Richard Allen and Absalom Jones staged a walkout, creating the Free African Society to administer aid, economic support, and leadership development to newly freed Blacks in Philadelphia.[23] This led to the creation of the African Methodist Episcopal Church in 1787, which became the first independent Black denomination in the United States.

The relationship between churches and Black philanthropic organizations continued through the nineteenth and twentieth centuries. Amid outside hostility, the church became the center and refuge for Black life. When there were no schools, it was churches that pooled resources together to fund educational advancements. And it was inside the literal and figurative walls of the church that Black men and some Black women achieved the distinction and status that inspired them to change their world.

Today, Black churches continue to be deeply involved in the community, addressing a multitude of challenges that impact their congregants—except one.

According to a recent Pew Research study, only 22 percent of Black churchgoers said they'd heard a message on abortion, compared to 34 percent of churchgoers across the nation.[24] If faithful preaching is not delivered on this topic, congregations will not see abortion as the same kind of travesty against human life as unsafe schools or gun violence.

Life matters to God at every turn, every stage, every crossroad. In this new fight for life, church leaders have an opportunity to teach a compassionate, comprehensive view that the world rarely offers, combatting the binary messages provided in the realm of politics. With Black women having the highest abortion rates, and with evidence of increased acceptance of abortion over the last fifteen years,[25] it is imperative that Black ministers, Black believers, and Black pro-life individuals speak truth. I understand that for the Black community, this isn't just a rejection of abortion or an endorsement of religion; it's about responding to immediate needs for survival. I believe we have the fortitude to address all this. And for our future, we must.

Of course, many churches are already doing this work faithfully. The Church of God in Christ, the nation's largest

Black denomination, with more than 6.5 million members worldwide, affirmed their pro-life stance in a 2019 resolution, stating, "The Church of God in Christ denounces the systematic destruction of human life by way of abortion." They went on to say that the denomination "believes in and supports the sanctity of human life."[26] Not only have they made and reaffirmed this statement, but they've also committed to a strategy that includes abstinence education, Bible-based sexual education, postabortion care, and funding for women's health care, including the construction of the Kingdom World Missions Center, a 100,000-square-foot building that provides financial help, food, and housing for women who choose life.[27]

Many churches offer both prenatal and postnatal services to Black women, who are frequently neglected by the US health care system. Others have helped women in crisis pregnancies access adoption options.[28]

While the media amplifies the voices of abortion supporters, many Black Christian women are reclaiming their pro-life heritage, protecting the lives of children in their care and pushing back against the misconception that pro-choice equals pro-women. They are willing to refute disingenuous factions of the conservative pro-life movement while still affirming that life is sacred.

The Whole Life Committee, for example, is a collection of nearly thirty Black women who are seeking to create a society that supports quality of life for mother and child, from womb to tomb. They work toward this goal by addressing poverty, maternal mortality, health care, and childcare. Relying on the Holy Spirit and harnessing the power of their own stories, they are exposing the lies of the abortion industry and proving the power of God to fix what has been broken.

In many respects, their work embodies the sentiments of Dr. Charlie Dates, lead pastor of Chicago's Progressive Baptist Church and Salem Baptist Church. He says,

> We are so caught up arguing over the finer points of abortion that we've not even exercised our power in eliminating the need for abortion. We wouldn't have to argue over whether or not abortions should exist if we would actually take care of women in the first place. If we would act like women deserve a livable wage, that childcare ought to be available, that kids deserve a chance at a real education. You don't have to beg a woman to keep her baby if you will be there to support the woman and act like she is made in the image and likeness of God.[29]

If more churches and pastors spoke with this kind of clarity and boldness, we just might be able to take a stronger stand for life in this country.

Shortly before the *Dobbs* decision was announced, the pastor at my church, Gilbert Kelly, preached a poignant message on abortion, offering a truthful representation of the complexities of this issue in America. Standing before a predominantly Black congregation, he upheld the dignity of the human image bearer in the womb, addressed the multiple economic pathways that lead to abortion decisions, called men to be the leaders we were created to be, and challenged the God-ordained institutions of church and government to serve, protect, and care for women and children.

As he spoke on a divisive issue during a highly politicized season in a deeply divided state, his sermon transcended politics and addressed the heart of the matter.

"[While] preparing this message," he began, "I asked God a rhetorical question . . . 'Would you be pro-choice, or would you be pro-life?' and God gave me an unexpected answer . . . 'Both.'"

The church was packed to capacity, but you could have heard a pin drop.

"God is the author of life; God is *not* the author of death," he continued. "God gave man the power to choose which voices to believe and to follow. . . . [In the beginning,] man chose to listen to the wrong voice, and the consequences of that choice were devastating. And when man makes the wrong choice today, the consequences [are] still devastating."

He looked out at the congregation and said emphatically, "God is pro-life. And God is pro-choice. But nowhere in his Word do I see where God is pro-abortion. . . . By the Word of God, abortion is wrong—in all cases."

Amid the swirling controversy over pro-choice and pro-life, he reminded us, "God gave us the power to choose, but he says, 'Choose life.'" In the end, "The most important question for us as believers is what will we do with the answer."[30]

When he finished, the reaction was not one of shock or awe.

It was simply this: "Amen."

THE BEGINNING OF THE END

*I have one life and one chance to make it count for something . . .
My faith demands that I do whatever I can, wherever I am,
whenever I can, for as long as I can with whatever I have to
try to make a difference.*

JIMMY CARTER

"*Roe* is DONE!!"

I posted those three simple words to social media on
June 24, 2022. The words had a celebratory note to them,
but they carried a measure of complexity and heaviness I was
unprepared to fully embrace.

"*Roe* is done" meant elation and hostility, joy and fear,
yesterday and tomorrow. It was simultaneously the anticipation of a new day, watching the morning haze start to clear,
and the uncertainty of dusk, seeing the waning sun disappear
beyond the horizon.

By now the cheers have faded, and although lives are
being rescued, I daresay a degree of apathy has descended
on some of those committed to the pro-life cause. When

the Supreme Court repealed *Roe v. Wade*, they assumed the game was over—we had won, and there was no more reason to fight.

That couldn't be further from the truth. The game is not over. And while we have won a significant battle, there is still a war going on. Lives are being lost. Now is not the time to sit back and rest on our laurels. If there was ever a time to refocus, reimagine, retool, and reboot the pro-life movement, the time is now.

HALFTIME ADJUSTMENTS

The game of football has left an indelible mark on me. Although I no longer play professionally, I still watch it, talk about it, and think about it. As a child, I was the kid who always wanted to go out and throw the ball with my dad or pull together a game with my friends on any patch of unoccupied grass or pavement we could find.

After sixteen years in the league, I sometimes reminisce about the locker room after a victory—the music, the shouting, the sense of accomplishment. I also recall walking into the locker room countless times for halftime. While the mood after the game was characterized by elation or defeat, at halftime the room was weighed down by the task at hand. Whether we were ahead by two touchdowns, behind by three, or deadlocked in a tie, the coaches took those twelve minutes to strategize for the adversity that awaited us in the second half.

In the first half, your first fifteen plays as a team are scripted. But when you return to the field for the second half, you know more about your opponent. You understand their game plan. You know exactly who they are, what they're trying to do, and how they're planning to do it. And they know the same about you.

Winning teams craft second-half plans that emphasize what has gone well, correct what has failed, and anticipate a winning response to their opponent's adjustments.

Make no mistake: second-half football is not for the faint of heart. The intensity increases, the opposition mounts, and fatigue attempts to make cowards of even the greatest champions. Yet victory awaits those who have the fortitude to overcome—together.

In this fight for life, we are now at halftime.

What happened in the Supreme Court didn't end abortion. It just sent the issue back to the states. Abortion is still legal in many places, and the same economic and relational factors that drove women to get abortions and drove men to push their girlfriends or wives to get abortions in the past are still in play. That's why overturning *Roe* can't be the end goal for a movement that claims to love life. This shift in jurisprudence is only a step, albeit a crucial one, along the way. The true goal is to make abortion unthinkable and unnecessary.

Making abortion *unthinkable* will require a change in the mindset, expectations, and sensibilities of our nation. It means creating a culture that values and supports motherhood so that pregnancy is seen no longer as an ending but a beginning. It will require deprogramming and reconstructing a national consciousness that has been conditioned to accept this evil as normal.

Making abortion *unnecessary* means knocking down the

barriers that obstruct a woman's view of her future as a parent by providing the resources and support that make choosing life a viable option. This will require a holistic effort at every level of society, repairing systems that drive women—particularly Black women—to believe they have no other choice.

I wrote this book for several reasons.

I wrote because it's imperative that those of us who stand for life understand how accessible abortion still is in the post-*Roe* landscape and what continues to hang in the balance. Roughly 75 percent of states still allow abortion. Even though a dozen states have fifteen- to twenty-four-week restrictions,[1] more than 90 percent of abortions occur before the first thirteen weeks of gestation.[2] *Roe* is done, but that does not end the killing.

I wrote because I couldn't bear to hear another talking point about abortion rates among Black women without hearing a subsequent point that unpacks the ugly, inconvenient, and uncomfortable reasons why. I've had enough of the veiled slander directed at our mothers, wives, sisters, and daughters. It's time to tell the whole story.

I wrote because I believe that justice is the connecting point that will unite the different factions of the pro-life movement, establish rapport and validity with those on the fringes, and—hopefully—foster a measure of respect from opponents. Ignorance of or disregard for racial justice—especially by some white pro-life evangelicals—has been a hurdle to unifying and expanding the movement. This may seem inconsequential, but it is not a side issue. Even more preborn children would be saved if justice for their mothers and fathers were a priority instead of an afterthought.

Finally, I wrote to refute the myth that the pro-life movement is all white and conservative. I wanted to challenge others to seek direction and leadership from the Black community and to implore churches—especially Black churches—to take a more active role in the fight for life.

In the face of other injustices over the course of history, Black men and women of faith have led, informed, demonstrated, and directed America, shaking it out of its reluctance to do right. We need to remember who we are.

It was Black Christians like Nat Turner who fought for their own manumission. It was Black Christians like Phillis Wheatley who spoke against the evils of slavery with an eloquent pen. It was Black Christians in Black churches who organized, strategized, and mobilized in the civil rights era. And it will be Black Christians and Black churches that will make the most important shifts to redress and protect Black lives from womb to tomb.

When it comes to abortion, I am convinced that Black believers in America are uniquely positioned to be the conscience of this nation—in part, because it impacts our community disproportionately. But I also believe that unity on this issue will evoke the power of God in ways we can't begin to imagine.

The body of Christ must never grow weary in doing good, because God has moved already—and he will continue to move. The church, empowered by the Spirit of God, has always been the leading voice for the voiceless. It will continue to be the catalyst that ignites others to protect God's image bearers on earth.

──────────────

Life secured a monumental victory in 2022, the result of decades of advocacy and sacrifice. But the new fight for life will look different from the way it looked in the first half. Our work will undoubtedly take more out of us than it did before.

We will have to reimagine and reinvent. We will have to build alliances that we once considered anathema. We will have to focus on the pathways that lead to abortion even more than the decision itself. And we will have to be open to God using us in ways we never thought possible.

Roe is done. And for that, we rejoice.

But the new fight for life is just getting started.

ACKNOWLEDGMENTS

This book was not an easy one to write. Life, justice, and race are interconnected lightning-rod issues that spark a wide range of emotions. Writing about all three faithfully, honestly, purposefully, and transparently challenged me in ways I did not expect.

At the beginning of this process, my wife sent me this verse: "Justice is a joy to the godly, but it terrifies evildoers" (Proverbs 21:15).

Kirsten, thank you for being sensitive to the Spirit, encouraging me with the words he gives you specifically for my time of need, and warmly embracing me when I feel inadequate. Thank you for covering me in prayer without ceasing and for walking this tightrope with me. I love you, babe.

Grace, Naomi, Isaiah, Judah, Eden, Asher, and Levi, thank you for cheering for Daddy in all things. Your excitement in watching me embark on new endeavors has motivated me along the way. I love all of you dearly.

Thank you to my writer, Carol Traver, for taking this

plunge with me into the deep water. I do not know how we brought this project together so quickly, but it would not have happened without your diligence and willingness to fully immerse yourself in my swirling thoughts and organize them for this acute purpose. What a journey.

Thank you to the entire Tyndale Momentum team for your continued enthusiasm and engagement with another Watson project. Your ideas and challenges have made the process of vision casting, brainstorming, and writing both enjoyable and fruitful.

Thank you to my literary agent, DJ Snell, for patiently yet persistently nudging me, conversing about the possibilities until this message became clear.

After I retired from the NFL, God used several people to guide me through what proved to be a confusing and cloudy period in my life. Thank you, DJ Jordan, for the hours you spent with me on the phone, helping me discover the passions and purposes God was placing on my heart. Your selfless actions made a greater impact than you know. Similarly, I must thank Randy Alcorn for sitting with me and offering godly wisdom on numerous occasions, and for demonstrating a commitment to life and justice.

Thank you to my Human Coalition family for your tireless work for life and for allowing me to serve with you. The last couple of years have been invaluable, as witnessing your efforts has expanded my understanding of what it means to serve women and children.

Over the last several years, I have had the opportunity to visit many pregnancy resource centers across this nation. A special thank-you to the countless individuals (and churches) who lead and support these critical organizations as they extend love and assistance to the mothers who come through their doors. From coast to coast, you have welcomed me during our brief time together.

There are several women who have inspired me in this space as they lead others to love *all* life. Thank you, Reverend Harriet Bradley, for the words you spoke to Kirsten and me about disrupting pathways that lead to abortion while creating pathways for mother and child to thrive. We hardly knew each other, but you were right on time. Thank you, Senator Katrina Jackson, Cherilyn Holloway, and Christina Bennett, for your interaction, input, and advice on different aspects of this project. I greatly appreciate your willingness to share your views and experiences with me over the last several years. Thank you, Elizabeth Graham and Carole Novielli, for answering my inquiries and providing crucial data that made this book possible.

Most important, I praise God, from whom all blessings flow. Thank you, Lord, for leading, guiding, and protecting my family and me through a challenging season of change. May your power be the source of our courage, and may your joy be our strength. Continue to establish the work of my hands.

NOTES

INTRODUCTION: THE END OF THE BEGINNING

1. MSNBC (@MSNBC), "BREAKING: U.S. SUPREME COURT OVERTURNS ROE V. WADE," Twitter, June 24, 2022, 9:35 a.m., https://twitter.com/msnbc/status/1540342868698603522.

2. Shannon Bream (@ShannonBream), "Dobbs opinion makes it official," Twitter, June 24, 2022, 9:21 a.m., https://twitter.com/ShannonBream /status/1540339340181659650.

3. ABC News (@ABC), "26 states are expected," Twitter, June 24, 2022, 9:43 a.m., https://twitter.com/abc/status/1540344784912613377?lang=en.

4. Josh Gerstein and Alexander Ward, "Supreme Court Has Voted to Overturn Abortion Rights, Draft Opinion Shows," *Politico*, May 2, 2022, https:// www.politico.com/news/2022/05/02/supreme-court-abortion-draft-opinion -00029473.

5. Aaron Blake, "What Ruth Bader Ginsburg Really Said about Roe v. Wade," *Washington Post*, June 27, 2022, https://www.washingtonpost.com/politics /2022/06/27/what-ruth-bader-ginsburg-really-said-about-roe-v-wade/.

6. Gerstein and Ward, "Supreme Court Has Voted to Overturn."

7. Justin McCarthy, "Record-High 70% in U. S. Support Same-Sex Marriage," Gallup, June 8, 2021, https://news.gallup.com/poll/350486/record-high -support-same-sex-marriage.aspx.

8. David Masci et al., "A History of Key Abortion Rulings of the U.S. Supreme Court," Pew Research Center, January 16, 2013, https://www .pewresearch.org/religion/2013/01/16/a-history-of-key-abortion-rulings -of-the-us-supreme-court/.

9. Michael Foust, "Tony Evans Urges Christians to Promote a 'Womb to the Tomb' Strategy for Pregnant Women," Christian Headlines, June 27, 2022, https://www.christianheadlines.com/contributors/michael-foust /tony-evans-urges-christians-to-promote-a-womb-to-the-tomb-strategy-for -pregnant-women.html.

10. Sam Matthews, "Self-Described 'Pro-Life Feminist': 'We're Not Ready to Overturn Roe,'" Yahoo! News, May 9, 2022, https://news.yahoo.com/self -described-pro-life-feminist-were-not-ready-to-overturn-roe-172025614 .html.

11. David French, "The Pro-Life Movement's Work Is Just Beginning," *Atlantic*, June 24, 2022, emphasis added, https://www.theatlantic.com /ideas/archive/2022/06/pro-life-dobbs-roe-culture-of-life/661394/.

12. Ericka Andersen, "'Greater Level of Desperation': As COVID-19 Rages, Pregnancy Centers See Surge in Demand," *USA Today*, August 9, 2020, https://www.usatoday.com/story/opinion/2020/08/09/covid-19-creates -desperation-women-turn-pregnancy-centers-column/3316935001/.

CHAPTER 1: THE ELEPHANT IN THE ROOM

1. Jessica Campisi and Brandon Griggs, "Of the 115 Supreme Court Justices in US History, All but Seven Have Been White Men," CNN, March 24, 2022, https://www.cnn.com/2022/03/24/politics/supreme-court-justices -minorities-cec/index.html.

2. "Ketanji Brown Jackson Becomes First Black Woman to Serve as a Justice of the U.S. Supreme Court," Death Penalty Information Center, July 5, 2022, https://deathpenaltyinfo.org/news/ketanji-brown-jackson-becomes -first-black-woman-to-serve-as-a-justice-of-the-u-s-supreme-court.

3. Carole Novielli, "The Beginning: How Planned Parenthood Became an Abortion Corporation," Live Action News, April 5, 2018, https://www .liveaction.org/news/how-planned-parenthood-abortion-corporation/.

4. Benjamin Watson, "Becoming People Who Are Pro-Life and Pro-Justice," Ethics and Religious Liberty Commission, 2018, https://erlc.com /resource-library/spotlight-articles/becoming-people-who-are-pro-life -and-pro-justice/.

5. Amethyst Holmes, "Pro-Life Black Christians Don't Focus on Abortion Alone," *Christianity Today*, June 29, 2022, https://www.christianitytoday .com/news/2022/june/pro-life-black-church-roe-v-wade-abortion-racism -whole-life.html.

6. W. E. B. Du Bois, *The Souls of Black Folk* (New York: Dover Publications, 1994), 2.

7. Samuel Smith, "NFL Star Ben Watson: We Must Teach 'Life Begins at Conception,'" *Christian Post*, December 28, 2016, https://www.christian post.com/news/nfl-star-ben-watson-we-must-teach-life-begins-at-conception .html.

8. "Ben Watson Speech at the March for Life Rally," January 27, 2017, video, 05:30, https://www.youtube.com/watch?v=n3rI88eFsLY.

9. Lauren Holter, "The Best States for Reproductive Rights," Bustle, July 20, 2015, https://www.bustle.com/articles/98424-the-4-best-states-for -reproductive-rights-are-where-we-should-all-move-stat.

10. Karen Ingle, "Football Star Benjamin Watson Equips Maryland Pregnancy Clinic to Defend Life," Pregnancy Help News, August 7, 2018, https://pregnancyhelpnews.com/football-star-benjamin-watson-equips-maryland-pregnancy-clinic-to-defend-life.

11. Katie Reilly, "A New York Law Has Catapulted Later Abortion Back into the Political Spotlight. Here's What the Legislation Actually Does," *Time*, February 1, 2019, https://time.com/5514644/later-abortion-new-york-law/.

12. Caleb Parke, "Illinois Bill Will Make State the 'Abortion Capital of America,' Pro-Life Group Warns," Fox News, February 25, 2019, https://www.foxnews.com/politics/illinois-abortion-bill-will-make-state-the-abortion-capital-of-america-pro-life-group-warns.

13. *Divided Hearts of America*, directed by Chad Bonham (Exploration Films, 2020), https://www.amazon.com/Divided-Hearts-America-Dr-Carson/dp/B09KYJH4RC/.

CHAPTER 2: A BRIEF HISTORY OF INJUSTICE

1. "The National Memorial for Peace and Justice," EJI, accessed November 20, 2022, https://museumandmemorial.eji.org/memorial.

2. Clint Smith, *How the Word Is Passed: A Reckoning with the History of Slavery across America* (New York: Little, Brown, 2021), 179.

3. Smith, 68.

4. Jesse Jackson, "How We Respect Life Is the Overriding Moral Issue," Right to Life News, January 1977, Project MAC, MIT Project on Mathematics and Computation, https://groups.csail.mit.edu/mac/users/rauch/nvp/consistent/jackson.html.

5. "Black Leaders during Reconstruction," History.com, updated August 25, 2022, https://www.history.com/topics/american-civil-war/black-leaders-during-reconstruction.

6. Alan Greenblatt, "The Racial History of the 'Grandfather Clause,'" Code Switch, NPR, October 22, 2013, https://www.npr.org/sections/codeswitch/2013/10/21/239081586/the-racial-history-of-the-grandfather-clause.

7. "Jim Crow Laws," History.com, updated January 11, 2022, https://www.history.com/topics/early-20th-century-us/jim-crow-laws.

8. David H. Gans, "The 14th Amendment Was Meant to Be a Protection against State Violence," *Atlantic*, July 19, 2020, https://www.theatlantic.com/ideas/archive/2020/07/14th-amendment-protection-against-state-violence/614317/.

9. Lisa Camner McKay, "How the Racial Wealth Gap Has Evolved—and Why It Persists," Federal Reserve Bank of Minneapolis, October 3, 2022, https://www.minneapolisfed.org/article/2022/how-the-racial-wealth-gap-has-evolved-and-why-it-persists.

10. Ana Patricia Muñoz et al., "The Color of Wealth in Boston," Federal Reserve Bank of Boston, March 25, 2015, https://www.bostonfed.org /publications/one-time-pubs/color-of-wealth.aspx.

11. Liz Mineo, "Racial Wealth Gap May Be a Key to Other Inequities," Harvard Gazette, June 3, 2021, https://news.harvard.edu/gazette/story /2021/06/racial-wealth-gap-may-be-a-key-to-other-inequities/; Kriston McIntosh et al., "Examining the Black-White Wealth Gap," *Up Front* (blog), Brookings, February 27, 2020, https://www.brookings.edu /blog/up-front/2020/02/27/examining-the-black-white-wealth -gap/.

12. Timothy Keller, *Generous Justice: How God's Grace Makes Us Just* (New York: Riverhead Books, 2012).

13. International Justice Mission (IJM), accessed November 22, 2022, https:// www.ijm.org/.

14. "Sex Trafficking," IJM, accessed November 22, 2022, https://www.ijm.org /our-work/trafficking-slavery/sex-trafficking.

15. Tim Keller, "What Is Biblical Justice?" *Relevant*, August 23, 2012, https:// relevantmagazine.com/faith/what-biblical-justice/.

16. Matt Haines, "Effects of Jim Crow Era Live On in Modern America, Some Say," Voice of America (VOA), April 22, 2021, https://www.voanews.com /a/usa_effects-jim-crow-era-live-modern-america-some-say/6204908 .html.

17. "Working Together to Reduce Black Maternal Mortality," Office of Minority Health and Health Equity, Centers for Disease Control and Prevention, April 6, 2022, https://www.cdc.gov/healthequity/features /maternal-mortality/index.html.

18. "Single Mother Statistics," Single Mother Guide (SMG), updated March 12, 2022, https://singlemotherguide.com/single-mother-statistics/.

19. James Studnicki, John W. Fisher, and James L. Sherley, "Perceiving and Addressing the Pervasive Racial Disparity in Abortion," *Health Services Research and Managerial Epidemiology* 7 (August 18, 2020): 2333392820949743, https://www.ncbi.nlm.nih.gov/pmc/articles/PMC7436774/.

20. David C. Reardon, "Women Who Abort: Their Reflections on Abortion," Elliot Institute, AfterAbortion.com, https://afterabortion.org/women -who-abort-their-reflections-on-abortion/; *USA Today*, August 9, 2020, https://www.usatoday.com/story/opinion/2020/08/09/covid-19-creates -desperation-women-turn-pregnancy-centers-column/3316935001/.

21. "The Demographics of Abortion in America," The Ethics and Religious Liberty Commission of the Southern Baptist Convention, May 6, 2022, https://www.cdc.gov/mmwr/volumes/71/ss/ss7110a1.htm#T6_down.

22. Langston Hughes, "Justice," in *The Collected Poems of Langston Hughes*, eds. Arnold Rampersad and David E. Roessel (New York: Vintage Books, 1995), 31.

23. Richard Rothstein, *The Color of Law: A Forgotten History of How Our Government Segregated America* (New York: Liveright Publishing, 2018), xv–xvi.

CHAPTER 3: A QUESTION OF HUMAN DIGNITY

1. James Studnicki, John W. Fisher, and James L. Sherley, "Perceiving and Addressing the Pervasive Racial Disparity in Abortion," *Health Services Research and Managerial Epidemiology* 7 (August 18, 2020): 2333392820949743, https://www.ncbi.nlm.nih.gov/pmc/articles/PMC7436774/.

2. Abort73.com, "Abortion and Race," Loxafamosity Ministries, last updated July 9, 2020, https://abort73.com/abortion/abortion_and_race.

3. John Piper, "When Is Abortion Racism?" Desiring God, January 21, 2007, https://www.desiringgod.org/messages/when-is-abortion-racism.

4. Elizabeth Nix, "Tuskegee Experiment: The Infamous Syphilis Study," History.com, updated December 15, 2020, https://www.history.com /news/the-infamous-40-year-tuskegee-study.

5. Nix.

6. Harriet A. Washington, *Medical Apartheid: The Dark History of Medical Experimentation on Black Americans from Colonial Times to the Present* (New York: Harlem Moon, 2008), 6.

7. "Black Americans Are Systematically Under-Treated for Pain. Why?" from Sophie Trawalter, "Racial Bias and Healthcare," June 24, 2020, *Batten Expert Chats*, Frank Batten School of Leadership and Public Policy, UVA, https://batten.virginia.edu/about/news/black-americans-are-systematically -under-treated-pain-why.

8. Vidya Rao, "'You Are Not Listening to Me': Black Women on Pain and Implicit Bias in Medicine," *Today*, July 27, 2020, https://www.today.com /health/implicit-bias-medicine-how-it-hurts-black-women-t187866.

9. "Working Together to Reduce Black Maternal Mortality," Office of Minority Health and Health Equity, Centers for Disease Control and Prevention, April 6, 2022, https://www.cdc.gov/healthequity/features /maternal-mortality/index.html.

10. John Kelly, Christopher Schnaars, and Alison Young, "Hospitals Blame Moms When Childbirth Goes Wrong. Secret Data Suggest It's Not That Simple," *USA Today*, March 7, 2019, https://www.usatoday.com/in-depth /news/investigations/deadly-deliveries/2019/03/07/maternal-death-rates -secret-hospital-safety-records-childbirth-deaths/2953224002/.

11. Women and the American Story, "Life Story: Anarcha, Betsy, and Lucy," New-York Historical Society, https://wams.nyhistory.org/a-nation-divided /antebellum/anarcha-betsy-lucy/; James Marion Sims, *The Story of My Life* (New York: D. Appleton and Company, 1894); and "The Mothers of Gynecology Monument," More Up Campus, accessed November 26, 2022, https://www.anarchalucybetsey.org/.

12. Chuck Reece, "Fanny Lou Hamer's America: A Primer," Bitter Southerner, accessed November 26, 2022, https://bittersoutherner.com/southern -perspective/2020/fannie-lou-hamer-a-primer.

13. "Elaine Riddick's Forced Sterilization Testimony," Amen Ptah, video, 3:45, https://www.youtube.com/watch?v=cFJNX5bHYVI.

14. "Elaine Riddick's Forced Sterilization Testimony."

15. David Zucchino, "Sterilized by North Carolina, She Felt Raped Once More," *Los Angeles Times*, January 25, 2012, https://www.latimes.com/archives/la -xpm-2012-jan-25-la-na-forced-sterilization-20120126-story.html.

16. Sara Kugler, "Mississippi Appendectomies and Reproductive Justice," MSNBC, March 25, 2014, http://www.msnbc.com/msnbc/day-17 -mississippi-appendectomies.

17. John D. Rockefeller, "The Trend of Things," *Charities and the Commons: A Weekly Journal of Philanthropy and Social Advance*, no. 21 (1908): 731, quoted in William A. Schambra, "Philanthropy's Original Sin," *New Atlantis*, Summer 2013, https://www.thenewatlantis.com/publications /philanthropys-original-sin.

18. "Eugenics," History.com, last updated January 13, 2021, https://www .history.com/topics/germany/eugenics.

19. "American Eugenics and the Nazi Regime: The Eugenics Crusade," U.S. History Collection, PBS Learning Media, https://gpb.pbslearningmedia .org/resource/amex32ec-soc-eugenicsnazi/american-eugenics-and-the-nazi -regime-the-eugenics-crusade/.

20. Kyle Morris and Sam Dorman, "Over 63 Million Abortions Have Occurred in the US Since *Roe v. Wade* Decision in 1973," Fox News, May 4, 2022, https://www.foxnews.com/politics/abortions-since-roe -v-wade.

21. Alana Varley, "Founder of Planned Parenthood Liked Sterilization, Hated Pregnancy Centers," *Abundant Life Blog*, CareNet, January 11, 2018, https://www.care-net.org/abundant-life-blog/margaret-sanger -unintelligent-people-are-a-drain-on-society-0-0-0.

22. Maria McFadden Maffucci, "The 'Poisonous Fruit' of Planned Parenthood," *Human Life Review*, April 23, 2021, https://humanlifereview.com/the -poisonous-fruit-of-planned-parenthood/.

23. Martin Luther King Jr., "The American Dream," in *A Knock at Midnight: Inspiration from the Great Sermons of Reverend Martin Luther King, Jr.*, ed. Clayborne Carson and Peter Holloran (New York: IPM/Warner Books, 2000).

24. Christina Gough, "Total Revenue of All National Football League Teams from 2001 to 2021," Statista, September 7, 2022, https://www.statista .com/statistics/193457/total-league-revenue-of-the-nfl-since-2005/.

25. Firing Line with Margaret Hoover (@FiringLineShow), "I said, no, you know what, I'm not ready," Twitter, October 7, 2022, 8:26 a.m., https:

//twitter.com/FiringLineShow/status/1578376341875032065; Isaac
Schorr, "Representative Cori Bush Says Abortionist Went Through with
Procedure against Her Will," October 7, 2022, *National Review*, https://
www.nationalreview.com/news/representative-cori-bush-says-abortionist
-went-through-with-procedure-against-her-will/.

26. Aris Folley, "Bush Testifies before Congress about Racist Treatment Black
Birthing People Face during Childbirth, Pregnancy," *The Hill*, May 6,
2021, https://thehill.com/policy/healthcare/552250-bush-testifies-before
-congress-about-racist-treatment-black-birthing-people/.

27. Juan Mejia, Allie Yang, and Taigi Smith, "Black Christians Discuss How
Faith Informs Their Stances on Abortion," ABC News, March 15, 2021,
emphasis added, https://abcnews.go.com/US/black-christians-discuss-faith
-informs-stances-abortion/story?id=76398415.

CHAPTER 4: HAVE A LITTLE EMPATHY

1. Liam Stack, "3 Men on Death Row in Louisiana Sue over Solitary
Confinement," *New York Times*, March 30, 2017, https://www.nytimes
.com/2017/03/30/us/3-men-on-death-row-in-louisiana-sue-over-solitary
-confinement.html.

2. Daniele Selby, "How the 13th Amendment Kept Slavery Alive: Perspectives
from the Prison Where Slavery Never Ended," Innocence Project,
September 17, 2021, https://innocenceproject.org/13th-amendment-slavery
-prison-labor-angola-louisiana/.

3. Roby Chavez, "Aging Louisiana Prisoners Were Promised a Chance at Parole
after 10 Years," PBS NewsHour, November 26, 2021, https://www.pbs.org
/newshour/nation/aging-louisiana-prisoners-were-promised-a-chance-at
-parole-after-10-years-some-are-finally-free.

4. Selby, "Perspectives from the Prison."

5. Carole Novielli, "Recent Data Shows Us Who Is Having Most Abortions,
and It May Surprise You," Live Action News, December 27, 2021, https://
www.liveaction.org/news/data-having-abortions-surprise/.

6. Lisa Cannon Green, "Women Distrust Church on Abortion," Lifeway
Research, November 23, 2015, https://research.lifeway.com/2015/11/23
/women-distrust-church-on-abortion/.

7. Justin Giboney, Michael Wear, and Chris Butler, *Compassion (&) Conviction:
The AND Campaign's Guide to Faithful Civic Engagement* (Downers Grove,
IL: IVP, 2020).

CHAPTER 5: THE POWER OF ONE

1. Allison McCann et al., "Tracking the States Where Abortion Is Now
Banned," *New York Times*, updated November 23, 2022, https://www
.nytimes.com/interactive/2022/us/abortion-laws-roe-v-wade.html; Scott
Neuman, "How Companies Offering to Cover Travel for Out-of-State

Abortions Might Work," NPR, July 5, 2022, https://www.npr.org/2022/07/05/1109401395/abortion-out-of-state-travel-costs-companies-roe-v-wade.

2. Sarah McCammon, "Planned Parenthood Mobile Clinic Will Take Abortion to Red-State Borders," *All Things Considered*, NPR, October 3, 2022, https://www.npr.org/2022/10/03/1125797779/planned-parenthood-mobile-clinic-will-take-abortion-to-red-state-borders.

3. Steve Inskeep and Sarah McCammon, "The FDA Relaxes Controversial Restrictions on Access to Abortion Pill by Mail," *Morning Edition*, NPR, December 17, 2021, https://www.npr.org/2021/12/17/1065083161/the-fda-relaxes-controversial-restrictions-on-access-to-abortion-pill-by-mail.

4. Jessica Arons, "With Roe Overturned, What Comes Next for Abortion Rights?" American Civil Liberties Union (ACLU), June 24, 2022, https://www.aclu.org/news/reproductive-freedom/what-comes-next-abortion-rights-supreme-court.

5. Gloria Purvis, "Perspective: Stop Framing Abortion as the Solution to Black Women's Problems," *Deseret News*, July 4, 2022, https://www.deseret.com/2022/7/4/23182289/perspective-stop-framing-abortion-as-the-solution-to-black-womens-problems-roe-v-wade-supreme-court.

6. "U.S. Abortion Statistics," Abort73.com, accessed November 29, 2022, https://abort73.com/abortion_facts/us_abortion_statistics/.

7. Ericka Andersen, "'Greater Level of Desperation': As COVID-19 Rages, Pregnancy Centers See Surge in Demand," *USA Today*, August 9, 2020, https://www.usatoday.com/story/opinion/2020/08/09/covid-19-creates-desperation-women-turn-pregnancy-centers-column/3316935001/.

8. Tony Evans, "Never Give Up, Part 1," October 7, 2021, *The Urban Alternative*, podcast, Truth Network, https://www.truthnetwork.com/show/the-urban-alternative-tony-evans-phd/32337/.

9. DJ Jordan, "Building Bridges to Repair Brokenness with DJ Jordan," August 4, 2020, *Think Orphan*, episode 150, interview with Phil Darke and Rick Mortin, podcast, 1:01:36, https://thinkorphan.com/2020/08/04/episode-150-dj-jordan/.

10. Caleb Parke, "Virginia Couple Adopts after Viral Pro-Life Post Telling Expectant Mothers Not to Get Abortion," Fox News, October 25, 2019, https://www.foxnews.com/faith-values/couple-adopt-pro-life-abortion-baby.

11. Moira Gaul, "Fact Sheet: Pregnancy Centers—Serving Women and Saving Lives (2020 Study)," Charlotte Lozier Institute, July 19, 2021, https://lozierinstitute.org/fact-sheet-pregnancy-centers-serving-women-and-saving-lives-2020/.

12. "Abortion Is a Common Experience for U.S. Women, Despite Dramatic Declines in Rates," Guttmacher Institute, October 19, 2017, https://www

.guttmacher.org/news-release/2017/abortion-common-experience-us
-women-despite-dramatic-declines-rates.

13. "Healing Wounded Hearts with Post-Abortion Stress Recovery," Caring
Network, accessed November 29, 2022, https://www.caringnetwork.com
/our-work/healing-wounded-hearts.

14. Randy Alcorn, "There's a Fierce Spiritual Battle at the Heart of Abortion,"
Randy Alcorn's Blog, Eternal Perspective Ministries, July 22, 2022, https://
www.epm.org/blog/2022/Jul/22/spiritual-battle-heart-abortion.

15. John Lewis (@repjohnlewis), Twitter, July 26, 2016, 2:39 p.m., https://
twitter.com/repjohnlewis/status/758023941998776321?lang=en.

16. Justin Giboney, Michael Wear, and Chris Butler, *Compassion (&) Conviction:
The AND Campaign's Guide to Faithful Civic Engagement* (Downers Grove,
IL: IVP, 2020), 86.

17. "Jackson Promotes Love Life Amendment," *Ouachita Citizen*, October 7,
2020, https://www.hannapub.com/ouachitacitizen/news/local_state
_headlines/jackson-promotes-love-life-amendment/article_44b6e530-08cc
-11eb-ad58-832954c9167b.html. Also see "Love Life Constitutional
Amendment," Louisiana Right to Life, accessed November 29, 2022,
https://prolifelouisiana.org/lovelife.

18. "Pro-Life Democrat Katrina Jackson Partners with Save the Storks," *Christian
News Journal*, December 12, 2019, https://christiannewsjournal.com/pro-life
-democrat-katrina-jackson-partners-with-save-the-storks/#.Y4pF1cvMKUk.

19. Katrina Jackson, "Save the Storks: Pro-Life Democrat Katrina Jackson
Speaks at Stork Ball 2020," speech, Washington, DC, January 23, 2020,
video, 10:33, https://youtu.be/tWatHXWtcvE.

20. Katrina Jackson, "Senator Katrina Jackson: Meet the Pro-Life Democrat
Who Wrote Louisiana's Abortion Law," EWTN Pro-Life Weekly, July 3,
2020, video, 6:34, https://youtu.be/paF5TBJ2C6A.

21. Bryan Stevenson, *Just Mercy: A Story of Justice and Redemption* (New York:
Spiegel and Grau, 2015), 18.

22. Dana Bash and Bridget Nolan, "Rep. Lucy McBath Is Living Her Son's
Legacy," Emily's List, https://www.emilyslist.org/news/entry/rep.-lucy
-mcbath-is-living-her-sons-legacy; originally published at CNN, May 24,
2021, https://www.cnn.com/2021/05/23/politics/badass-women-lucy
-mcbath/index.html.

23. Cheyenne Haslett, "Lucy McBath, Lost Son to Gun Violence, Wins
Democratic Nomination in Georgia: 'To Not Do Anything Is a Tragedy,'"
ABC News, July 25, 2018, https://abcnews.go.com/Politics/tragedy-mom
-lost-son-gun-violence-wins-democratic/story?id=55350934.

24. Bash and Nolan, "Rep. Lucy McBath."

25. Adapted from Loren Eiseley, "The Star Thrower," in *The Unexpected
Universe* (New York: Harcourt Brace, 1969).

CHAPTER 6: THE ROOT OF THE PROBLEM

1. Martin Luther King Jr., *Where Do We Go from Here: Chaos or Community?* (Boston: Beacon Press, 1968), 109.
2. King, 11.
3. William A. Darity Jr. and A. Kirsten Mullen, *From Here to Equality: Reparations for Black Americans in the Twenty-First Century* (Chapel Hill: University of North Carolina Press, 2020), 264.
4. Ana Patricia Muñoz et al., "The Color of Wealth in Boston," Federal Reserve Bank of Boston, March 25, 2015, https://www.bostonfed.org /publications/one-time-pubs/color-of-wealth.aspx.
5. Rebecca Charles, Sophie Collyer, and Christopher Wimer, "The Role of Government Transfers in the Black-White Child Poverty Gap," *Poverty and Social Policy Brief* 6, no. 3 (March 2022), Center on Poverty and Social Policy at Columbia University, https://static1.squarespace.com /static/610831a16c95260dbd68934a/t/622a300c46e382698827a2f1 /1646932056576/Role-of-Government-Transfers-Black-White-Child -Poverty-Gap-CPSP-2022.pdf.
6. King, *Chaos or Community?*, 162.
7. Paul Meany, "Thomas Paine's Centuries-Old Argument for UBI as a Right," Basic Income Today, August 6, 2020, https://basicincometoday .com/thomas-paines-centuries-old-argument-for-ubi-as-a-right/.
8. Lorie Konish, "New Stimulus Proposals Look like a Guaranteed Income Experiment. Early Results Show Whether It Will Work," CNBC, March 7, 2021, https://www.cnbc.com/2021/03/07/will-us-experiments-with -guaranteed-income-work.html.
9. Megan Greenwell, "Universal Basic Income Has Been Tested Repeatedly. It Works. Will America Ever Embrace It?" *Washington Post*, October 24, 2022, https://www.washingtonpost.com/magazine/2022/10/24 /universal-basic-income/; Abhijit Banerjee, Paul Niehaus, and Tavneet Suri, "Universal Basic Income in the Developing World" (NBER Working Paper Series 25598, National Bureau of Economic Research, Cambridge, MA, 2019), 5, https://www.nber.org/system/files/working_papers/w25598 /w25598.pdf.
10. Sara Luterman, "Magnolia Mother's Trust Marks a History-Making Three Cycles of Paying Black Mothers $1,000 a Month," The 19th, August 19, 2022, https://19thnews.org/2022/08/magnolia-mothers-trust-guaranteed -income-black-mothers/.
11. Luterman.
12. Greenwell, "Universal Basic Income."
13. Nelson Mandela, "Africa Standing Tall against Poverty," speech, Live 8 concert, Mary Fitzgerald Square, Johannesburg, South Africa, July 2, 2005, https://atom.nelsonmandela.org/index.php/za-com-mr-s-753.
14. Greenwell, "Universal Basic Income."

15. Thabiti Anyabwile, "Reparations Are Biblical," *The Gospel Coalition* (blog), October 10, 2019, https://www.thegospelcoalition.org/blogs /thabiti-anyabwile/reparations-are-biblical/.

16. Emma García, "Schools Are Still Segregated, and Black Children Are Paying a Price," Economic Policy Institute (EPI), February 12, 2020, https://www.epi.org/publication/schools-are-still-segregated-and-black -children-are-paying-a-price/.

17. Jack Schneider, "What School-Funding Debates Ignore," *Atlantic*, January 22, 2018, https://www.theatlantic.com/education/archive/2018/01/what-school -funding-debates-ignore/551126/.

18. "Nonwhite School Districts Get $23 Billion Less than White Districts despite Serving the Same Number of Students," EdBuild, February 2019, https://edbuild.org/content/23-billion.

19. Anna North, "How School Funding Can Help Repair the Legacy of Segregation," Vox, February 17, 2021, https://www.vox.com/22266219 /biden-education-school-funding-segregation-antiracist-policy.

20. Rebecca Bellan, "$23 Billion Education Funding Report Reveals Less Money for City Kids," Bloomberg, March 27, 2019, https://www.bloomberg.com /news/articles/2019-03-27/why-city-kids-get-less-money-for-their-education.

21. Schneider, "What School-Funding Debates Ignore."

22. Kelly Musick et al., "Education Differences in Intended and Unintended Fertility," *Social Forces* 88, no. 2 (December 2009): 543–572, https://www .ncbi.nlm.nih.gov/pmc/articles/PMC3578704/.

23. Heini Väisänen, "The Association between Education and Induced Abortion for Three Cohorts of Adults in Finland," *Population Studies* 69, no. 3 (September 2, 2015): 373–388, https://www.ncbi.nlm.nih.gov/pmc /articles/PMC4950447/.

24. "Black Women Aren't Paid Fairly," Lean In, accessed December 4, 2022, https://leanin.org/data-about-the-gender-pay-gap-for-black-women.

25. Beth Ann Bovino et al., "How the Advancement of Black Women Will Build a Better Economy for All," S&P Global, June 8, 2021, https:// www.spglobal.com/en/research-insights/featured/special-editorial/how -the-advancement-of-black-women-will-build-a-better-economy-for-all.

26. North, "How School Funding Can Help."

27. North.

28. North.

29. "About Us," Human Dignity Curriculum, accessed December 4, 2022, https://humandignitycurriculum.org/about-us/.

30. Breck Giltner, "The HDC Is Our Hope," January 25, 2022, https://human dignitycurriculum.org/hdc-in-action/the-hdc-is-our-hope/.

31. Giltner.

32. C. Kirabo Jackson, Rucker C. Johnson, and Claudia Persico, "The Effects of School Spending on Educational and Economic Outcomes: Evidence from

School Finance Reforms" (NBER Working Paper Series 25598, National Bureau of Economic Research, Cambridge, MA, 2019), 3, https://www.nber.org/system/files/working_papers/w20847/w20847.pdf.

33. Meredith Kolodner, "Why Aren't Flagship Universities Enrolling More of Their Own States' Black Students?" NBC, September 28, 2022, https://www.nbcnews.com/news/nbcblk/arent-flagship-universities-enrolling-black-students-state-rcna48986.

34. Hannah Gross, "The Case for Affirmative Action in College Admissions," National Education Association, October 31, 2022, https://www.nea.org/advocating-for-change/new-from-nea/case-affirmative-action-college-admissions.

35. Gross.

36. Ashlee Banks, "The Black Mamas Matter Alliance Is Asking Chuck Schumer to Help with Workplace Discrimination," *Essence*, January 13, 2022, https://www.essence.com/news/black-mamas-matter-alliance-pregnant-workplace-discrimination/.

37. Banks.

38. "Pregnant Workers Fairness," A Better Balance, accessed December 4, 2022, https://www.abetterbalance.org/our-issues/pregnant-workers-fairness/.

39. Krystin Arneson, "The US Is the Only Rich Nation Offering No National Paid Parental-Leave Programme. Why Is That—and Could It Change?" Equality Matters, BBC, June 28, 2021, https://www.bbc.com/worklife/article/20210624-why-doesnt-the-us-have-mandated-paid-maternity-leave.

40. Arneson.

41. Nadine El-Bawab, "Employers Offer Stipends for Babysitting and Tutoring to Sweeten Child-Care Benefits and Win Over Workers, CNBC, July 9, 2021, https://www.cnbc.com/2021/07/09/employers-sweeten-child-care-benefits-to-win-over-workers-.html.

42. Paula Faris, *You Don't Have to Carry It All: Ditch the Mom Guilt and Find a Better Way Forward* (Nashville, TN: Worthy Books, 2023).

43. El-Bawab, "Employers Offer Stipends."

44. El-Bawab, "Employers Offer Stipends."

45. Planned Parenthood, *Here for a Reason: 2020–2021 Annual Report* (New York: Planned Parenthood Federation of America, 2020–2021), 28, 30, https://www.plannedparenthood.org/uploads/filer_public/40/8f/408fc2ad-c8c2-48da-ad87-be5cc257d370/211214-ppfa-annualreport-20-21-c3-digital.pdf.

46. "New Analysis Finds Planned Parenthood Facilities Outnumbered 14 to 1," Charlotte Lozier Institute, https://lozierinstitute.org/new-analysis-finds-planned-parenthood-facilities-outnumbered-14-to-1/.

47. "Planned Parenthood Announces $16 Million Paid Media Campaign on National Abortion Access Crisis Ahead of Supreme Court Decision,"

Planned Parenthood, April 27, 2022, https://www.plannedparenthood.org
/about-us/newsroom/press-releases/planned-parenthood-announces-16
-million-paid-media-campaign-on-national-abortion-access-crisis-ahead-of
-supreme-court-decision.

48. Carole Novielli, "'Maternity Care Deserts' Ignored in Favor of Expanding
Abortion Access," Live Action, November 26, 2022, https://www.live
action.org/news/maternity-care-deserts-ignored-abortion/.

49. "Considering Abortion," Planned Parenthood, accessed December 4, 2022,
https://www.plannedparenthood.org/learn/abortion/considering-abortion.

50. Charlotte Lozier Institute, https://lozierinstitute.org/.

51. Moira Gaul, "Fact Sheet: Pregnancy Centers—Serving Women and Saving
Lives (2020 Study)," Charlotte Lozier Institute, July 19, 2021, https://
lozierinstitute.org/fact-sheet-pregnancy-centers-serving-women-and-saving
-lives-2020/.

52. Novielli, "Maternity Care Deserts."

53. Novielli.

54. Novielli.

55. "Key Facts and Statistics," National Foster Care Month, Children's Bureau,
2022, https://www.childwelfare.gov/fostercaremonth/awareness/facts/.

56. "The Problem," Foster America, accessed December 4, 2022, https://www
.foster-america.org/the-problem.

57. *Divided Hearts of America*, directed by Chad Bonham (Exploration Films,
2020), https://www.amazon.com/Divided-Hearts-America-Dr-Carson/dp
/B09KYJH4RC/.

CHAPTER 7: THE BODY OF CHRIST

1. Anugrah Kumar, "Are Most Single Christians in America Having Sex?,"
Christian Post, September 28, 2011, https://www.christianpost.com/news
/are-most-single-christians-in-america-having-sex.html.

2. Elizabeth Wildsmith, Jennifer Manlove, and Elizabeth Cook, "Dramatic
Increase in the Proportion of Births outside of Marriage in the United States
from 1990 to 2016," Child Trends, August 8, 2018, https://www.childtrends
.org/publications/dramatic-increase-in-percentage-of-births-outside-marriage
-among-whites-hispanics-and-women-with-higher-education-levels.

3. Mo Isom, *Sex, Jesus, and the Conversations the Church Forgot* (Grand Rapids,
MI: Baker Books, 2018), chap. 1, e-book.

4. "Child Welfare and Foster Care Statistics," The Annie E. Casey Foundation,
updated September 26, 2022, https://www.aecf.org/blog/child-welfare-and
-foster-care-statistics.

5. "The Father Absence Crisis in America" (National Fatherhood Initiative:
Philadelphia, 2022), fatherhood.org, https://135704.fs1.hubspotusercontent
-na1.net/hubfs/135704/2022%20Strengths%20Based%20Infographics
/NFIFatherAbsenceInfoGraphic.pdf.

6. Isom, introduction to *Sex, Jesus, and the Conversations*.
7. Scott Gillenwaters, "Mentioning the Unmentionable: Sex Ed in the Church (Part 1)," Center for Youth Ministry Training, accessed December 8, 2022, https://www.cymt.org/mentioning-the-unmentionable-sex-ed-in-the -church-1/.
8. UW Medicine Harborview Abuse and Trauma Center, *Sexual Behavior and Children: When Is It a Problem and What to Do about It* (Seattle, WA: University of Washington School of Medicine, 2012), https://depts .washington.edu/uwhatc/PDF/TF-%20CBT/pages/3%20Psycho education/Child%20Sexual%20Behaviors/Sexual%20Behavior %20and%20Children.pdf.
9. Rob Jackson, "Sex Education for Kids Ages 9–12," Focus on the Family, January 24, 2020, https://www.focusonthefamily.com/parenting/sex -education-how-to-start-early/.
10. "How to Talk to Your Kids about Sex (Part 1 of 3)," Lifeway, January 1, 2014, https://www.lifeway.com/en/articles/talking-to-your-kids-about-sex -part-one.
11. Kevin "KB" Burgess, *Dangerous Jesus: Why the Only Thing More Risky than Getting Jesus Right Is Getting Jesus Wrong* (Carol Stream, IL: Tyndale Momentum, 2023), 37.
12. Rodney Stark, *The Rise of Christianity: A Sociologist Reconsiders History* (Princeton, NJ: Princeton University Press, 1996), 208.
13. Stark, *The Rise of Christianity*, 84.
14. Burgess, *Dangerous Jesus*, 14.
15. Russell Moore, *Onward: Engaging the Culture without Losing the Gospel* (Nashville: B&H, 2015), 88.
16. Moore, 181.
17. Moore, 8.
18. Joan Brunkard, Gonza Namulanda, and Raoult Ratard, "Hurricane Katrina Deaths, Louisiana, 2005," American Medical Association, August 28, 2008, https://ldh.la.gov/assets/docs/katrina/deceasedreports/KatrinaDeaths _082008.pdf.
19. Fred Luter, "Pro-Life Series: I'm Black, I'm Pro-Life, This Is Why," interview by Jonathan Burton, Louisiana Black Advocates for Life, Facebook, April 13, 2021, video, 1:03:18, https://www.facebook.com/lablackadvocates/videos /276128494050276.
20. "Abortion Is a Common Experience for U.S. Women, despite Dramatic Declines in Rates," Guttmacher Institute, October 19, 2017, https:// www.guttmacher.org/news-release/2017/abortion-common-experience -us-women-despite-dramatic-declines-rates.
21. Vince L. Bantu, introduction to *Gospel Haymanot: A Constructive Theology and Critical Reflection on African and Diasporic Christianity*, ed. Vince L. Bantu (Chicago: Urban Ministries, 2020), 35.

22. William A. Darity Jr. and A. Kirsten Mullen, *From Here to Equality: Reparations for Black Americans in the Twenty-First Century* (Chapel Hill: University of North Carolina Press, 2020), 9, 157–159.

23. "Richard Allen: One of America's Founding Fathers," The Constitutional Walking Tour of Philadelphia, July 2, 2020, https://www.theconstitutional .com/blog/2020/07/01/richard-allen-one-americas-founding-fathers.

24. Besheer Mohamed et al., "Religion and Politics," Pew Research Center, February 16, 2021, https://www.pewresearch.org/religion/2021/02/16 /religion-and-politics/.

25. Aallyah Wright, "Has the Black Church Evolved on Abortion?" Capital B, July 21, 2022, https://capitalbnews.org/black-churches-abortion-roe/.

26. General Assembly Resolution Committee, "Resolution on the Sanctity of Life," Church of God in Christ, Inc., November 2019, https://www.cogic .org/wp-content/uploads/2019/12/SOLife-Resolution-11_12_19-1.pdf.

27. "Church of God in Christ Reaffirms Pro-Life Stance," Church of God in Christ, Inc., January 21, 2022, https://www.cogic.org/blog/church-of-god -in-christ-reaffirms-pro-life-stance/.

28. Wright, "Has the Black Church Evolved on Abortion?"

29. "'Bring Him to Me' Guest Preacher Dr. Charlie Dates," sermon, October 30, 2022, First Baptist Church of Glenarden, Inside FBCG, November 5, 2022, video, 57:15, https://www.youtube.com/watch?v=DaNUlZIcU50 &feature=youtu.be.

30. Gilbert Kelly, "Abortion?," sermon, May 22, 2022, New City Church, video, 48:24, https://www.youtube.com/watch?v=BeYdiAk2nEg.

EPILOGUE: THE BEGINNING OF THE END

1. Megan Messerly, "Abortion Is Illegal in a Quarter of the Country Heading into Election Day," *Politico*, November 8, 2022, https://www.politico.com /news/2022/11/08/abortion-status-heading-into-election-day-00065273.

2. "CDCs Abortion Surveillance System FAQs," Reproductive Health, Centers for Disease Control and Prevention, last reviewed November 17, 2022, https://www.cdc.gov/reproductivehealth/data_stats/abortion.htm.

DISCUSSION QUESTIONS

INTRODUCTION

Do you remember where you were when you got the news that *Roe v. Wade* had been overturned? What was your reaction? What emotions did you experience?

What has your journey been when it comes to issues of life? What experiences and influences have shaped your views and convictions?

CHAPTER 1

What do you think it means to be pro-life? Why do you think this topic tends to be defined rather narrowly?

How much freedom do you feel to speak out on the issue of abortion? What tends to hold you back? Who do you think has the right and the responsibility to speak into this topic?

CHAPTER 2

How would you define justice? Do you think there are absolutes when it comes to justice?

What injustices do you see in our world today? How do these injustices compare to injustices in previous generations?

What are the implications when justice becomes merely about politics? What role do you think politics should play in the quest for justice?

CHAPTER 3

Have your experiences with the medical community led to a sense of trust or distrust? In what ways has our country's history of exploitation led some individuals and communities to fight for greater autonomy?

In what ways does our society value performance over personhood? How have you personally felt the pressure of "What have you done for me lately?"

What does it mean to you that every person is created in the image of God? Practically speaking, how does this affect the way you treat other people and the way you view yourself?

CHAPTER 4

What experiences or people in your life have taught you about empathy? What are some ways we can pass on empathy to the next generation?

Who do you identify with in the story of the Good Samaritan? What do you think tends to get in the way of our being willing to help people on the proverbial side of the road?

CHAPTER 5

The author poses this question: "How will we fight for justice, disrupting the pathways that lead to abortion in the first place and slaying this evil at the source?" Why do you think it's important to address not just abortion itself but the root of the problem?

Consider the time, talent, and treasure God has entrusted to you. What gifts could you use to further the fight for life?

Which of the suggestions in this chapter have you implemented? Which ones come naturally for you, and which are more challenging? What are some additional ways people can get involved?

CHAPTER 6

The author says, "A true pro-life commitment to justice will require an intentional, strategic, precise effort to make right what has been wrong." Do you agree with this statement? Why or why not?

In order for lasting societal change to take place, it will require a concerted effort from the government, churches, and individuals. What role do you think each entity should play?

CHAPTER 7

What important role do men (and dads in particular) play in making abortion unthinkable and unnecessary?

The author says, "I believe the new fight for life is a spiritual battle." In what ways do you see that play out?

What new ideas are you considering after reading this book? What action steps do you plan to take after reading this book?

BENJAMIN WATSON is a former NFL tight end, as well as a writer, a speaker, and an activist. He is a college football studio analyst with the SEC Network, and he serves as VP of strategic relationships with the Human Coalition, one of the largest pro-life and pro-woman organizations in the country. Along with his wife, Kirsten, he is the founder of The Watson 7 Foundation, a nonprofit focused on strengthening families. They live in Georgia with their seven children.

CAROL TRAVER has been helping authors shape their stories for more than a decade. Her previous collaborative efforts include *Part of My World* by Disney legend Jodi Benson, *With My Eyes Wide Open* by KoRn guitarist Brian "Head" Welch, and *I'm No Angel* by former Victoria's Secret runway model Kylie Bisutti. She lives in the Chicago area.

THERE IS HOPE FOR HONEST AND HEALING CONVERSATION.

Get real about race with Benjamin Watson and the *Under Our Skin* experience.

Under Our Skin

After Ferguson, Benjamin Watson couldn't stay silent—and his comments took the Internet by storm. Now, in *Under Our Skin*, Watson honestly examines both sides of the race debate and appeals to the power and possibility of faith as a step toward healing.

Under Our Skin Group Conversation Guide

Based on the groundbreaking book *Under Our Skin*, this four-week guide for churches and small groups will foster honest conversation about race, bias, and justice in our nation.